D1557477

1968

1968

a Pivotal Moment
in American SPORTS

James C. Nicholson

SPORT and POPULAR CULTURE Brian M. Ingrassia, Series Editor

The University of Tennessee Press / Knoxville

*The Sport and Popular Culture series is designed to promote critical,
innovative research in the history of sport through a wide spectrum of works—
monographs, edited volumes, biographies, and reprints of classics.*

Library of Congress Cataloging-in-Publication Data
Names: Nicholson, James C., author.
Title: 1968: a pivotal moment in American sports / James C. Nicholson.
Other titles: Nineteen sixty-eight
Description: First edition. | Knoxville: University Tennessee Press, 2019.
| Series: Sports and popular culture | Includes bibliographical references and index. |
Identifiers: LCCN 2018040734 (print) | LCCN 2018054249 (ebook)
| ISBN 9781621905004 (Kindle) | ISBN 9781621905011 (pdf) | ISBN 9781621904991 (hardback)
Subjects: LCSH: Sports—United States—History—20th century.
| Sports—Social aspects—United States—History—20th century.
| Sports—Political aspects—United States—History—20th century.
| Nineteen sixty-eight, A.D. | BISAC: SPORTS & RECREATION / History.
| HISTORY / United States / 20th Century. | SPORTS & RECREATION / Golf.
| SPORTS & RECREATION / Boxing. | SPORTS & RECREATION / Baseball / History.
| SPORTS & RECREATION / Horse Racing. | SPORTS & RECREATION / Olympics.
Classification: LCC GV583 (ebook) | LCC GV583 .N43 2019 (print) | DDC 796.097309046—dc23
LC record available at https://lccn.loc.gov/2018040734

Contents

Foreword / Brian M. Ingrassia   ix

Acknowledgments   xiii

Introduction   1

prologue
December 31, 1967   5

CHAPTERS

one
Leap Year   7

two
Law and Order   31

three
Where Have You Gone . . . ?   55

four
Mexico City   81

five
Antiheroes   101

Epilogue   121

Notes   129

Index   145

Illustrations

Ice Bowl, Lambeau Field
6

Nguyen Ngoc Loan Executing
Viet Cong Prisoner
9

George Wallace, University
of Alabama, 1963
11

Lyndon B. Johnson Signing
Civil Rights Act of 1968
14

Soldiers at Capitol
17

Aftermath of Washington, DC, Riots
18

Muhammad Ali Knocks Out
Sonny Liston, 1965
26

Muhammad Ali with Howard Cosell,
Houston, 1967
29

Clifford Roberts, Masters Chairman
36

Roberto De Vicenzo, Bob Goalby
40

Peter Fuller, Bobby Ussery,
Dancer's Image, Lou Cavalaris
51

Robert Kennedy at
the Ambassador Hotel
58

Mickey Mantle
62

Violence at the
Democratic National Convention
65

Illinois Delegates React
to Sen. Abraham Ribicoff
67

Miss America Protesters
69

Detroit Riots
72

Hubert Humphrey Congratulates
Bob Gibson
76

Jose Feliciano
77

Avery Brundage, President of the
International Olympic Committee
87

Tommie Smith, John Carlos, and
Peter Norman on Olympic Podium
93

George Wallace Responds
to Heckling
102

Wallace-LeMay Campaign Buttons
103

Richard Nixon Throwing First Pitch
105

Joe Namath after Super Bowl III
111

Curt Flood
123

Muhammad Ali Funeral Procession
127

Foreword

"The whole world is watching."

Such was the mantra of demonstrators at the Democratic National Convention in Chicago, Illinois, in August 1968. They chanted their ominous refrain as television cameras rolled, catching police in the act of lashing out violently against anti-Vietnam War protesters in the late-summer heat. A half-century later, historians understand that 1968 was a year of global turmoil, especially in cities stretching from Chicago to Baltimore, from Paris to Prague. Helmeted gendarmes were battening the hatches of societies that appeared to be splitting apart at the seams. In April Martin Luther King Jr. was martyred by a white supremacist's bullet in Memphis, and in June Robert F. Kennedy succumbed to an assassin's bullet shortly after winning California's Democratic primary. It is no wonder Chicago saw such violence two months later. By November, Richard Nixon, Hubert Humphrey, and George Wallace battled for America's political soul, tearing the electoral map apart in ways most voters could not have anticipated when Lyndon Johnson was elected in a landslide just four years earlier.

Although it originated in politics, the immortal phrase, "the whole world is watching," may have applied just as well to sports in the turbulent 1960s. Journalists, with the traditional tools of their trade augmented by television cameras and satellites, facilitated the transformation of spectator sport into another terrain of combative cultural discourse. The playing field was becoming more like a minefield. In *1968: A Pivotal Moment in American Sports,* author James C. Nicholson encourages us to focus our attention on that year of assassinations and demonstrations, using sport as a lens to understand the emerging fault lines of American culture and society. We see a nation where many young people, including athletes, grew increasingly willing to challenge the status quo. However, we can also glimpse a nation clinging stubbornly to traditional mores. Nineteen sixty-eight was a year of turmoil in sport and popular culture not just because of innovative ideas and stances, but also because of widespread resistance to their implications. Analysis of 1968 sport reminds us that Nixon and Wallace were not the only ones stressing "law and order" or fomenting backlash. In places like Augusta, Boston, Louisville, and Mexico City, a hidebound generation turned back against any winds that augured change, urging adherence to rules that, at least to some, increasingly seemed unfair.

Nicholson is a talented writer who has published extensively on the history of horse racing, especially the Kentucky Derby. He has shown how the fabled "Run for the Roses" illuminates moments of *kairos* in American cultural history, the pivotal moments when the figurative turf shifted beneath society's collective feet (or hooves, as it may be). In *1968*, though, Nicholson broadens his focus to boxing, golf, baseball, and the Olympics, in addition to the race track. His quick-paced tour through one of the most turbulent sporting calendars on record inspires readers to see how in just one dramatic year American society simultaneously fractured and reshaped itself for a new kind of world that was then abandoning the post-1945 order. Cultural tectonic plates were shifting, and clearly not everyone was happy about it.

Athletic contests are, in many ways, about the enshrinement and following of rules. According to some definitions, sport is an unscripted physical drama acted out within the clear parameters of established conventions: rules regarding scorekeeping, player eligibility, treatment of opponents, or celebration of victory. Clearly, in an era of rampant protests and demonstrations, some Americans were unwilling to see those rules—or any rules, really—overturned. Nicholson relates the familiar story of Tommie Smith's and John Carlos's daring Black Power salute at the Mexico City Olympics in September, both men inspired by sociology professor Harry Edwards and the Olympic Project for Human Rights; he also recounts International Olympic Committee President Avery Brundage's predictable reaction. But *1968* digs deeper into the sporting annals of that year. In April, amiable Argentinian golfer Roberto De Vicenzo lost the Masters due to a slight yet irrevocable error on a scorecard. At the Kentucky Derby in May, controversy ensued after the apparent champion tested positive for a controlled substance. The powers that be were unwilling to budge. Things seemed to be changing too quickly, and the old guard was dedicated to maintaining order as long as possible.

The cast of characters in this story is nearly dizzying. For at least one year a tremendous array of consequential sports figures occupied adjacent and sometimes conflicting spaces in American sporting culture. Howard Cosell's incisive, cutting edge television commentary is part of the story, but so is Brent Musburger's reactionary piece on Smith and Carlos in the *Chicago American*. The World Series, populated by horsehide legends like Bob Gibson, Lou Brock, Denny McLain, and Mickey Lolich, gets its due, but we are reminded that perhaps the most divisive aspect of the 1968 Fall Classic may not have been the Gibson/McLain pitching matchup in games one and four; rather, it was Jose Feliciano's unorthodox rendition of the "Star Spangled Banner" before game five at Tiger Stadium. By today's standards the blind Puerto Rican folksinger's version of the national anthem is fairly benign, but at the time it inspired an angry backlash. And in that series Curt Flood—not yet famous as the John the Baptist of free agency—only garnered controversy by slipping on the wet centerfield grass at Busch Stadium.

The sporting world of 1968 may at first glance seem very different from that of the present, yet in many ways its issues and concerns echo into our own era. This book is a timely one. Smith's and Carlos's unshod feet and raised fists were meant to remind the whole world of racial injustice in the United States and beyond, but many of those watching at that time did not want to be aware. Muhammad Ali's refusal to step forward for induction when the name Cassius Clay was called was a way of protesting racism as well as the war in Vietnam, but in the year of Tet and Huế and Mỹ Lai, many observers just wanted to keep their blinders on. Reading Ali's story now, we cannot help but be reminded of knees taken during national anthems—usually sung in a manner somewhat more conventional than Feliciano's—or Department of Defense–funded fighter jets soaring over stadiums filled with waving flags and camouflage-clad players. When we watch, though, do we see the parallels to an earlier era of protest? Indeed, the words and actions of Chicago's Mayor Richard J. Daley in August 1968 reverberate and are amplified in the discourse of current American politicians who would lead us to make a nation great by returning to practices and conventions either long-since rejected or no longer appropriate for this world we call our own. There may, in short, be no better way to understand our turbulent present than by turning our attention to the sporting world of half a century ago—a world engulfed in controversies that many were watching but which some may not have comprehended.

Brian M. Ingrassia
West Texas A&M University

Acknowledgments

When I started to research this subject matter more than eight years ago, I thought that I would be telling a somewhat different story. But intervening shifts in the landscapes of American politics and sports cast the events of fifty years ago in a slightly different light. I am grateful for all of the help and encouragement I have received in developing this project and in getting it to the finish line.

Joanne Melish was the first person to inspire me to endeavor to write well. I may not have quite figured out how to do it, but my writing and I are both better for having known her. She convinced me that I could tackle this topic. Aram Goudsouzian helped me to conclude that I had found a story worth telling, and two anonymous reviewers made it a better book.

I appreciate the time and effort Thomas Wells, Tom Post, Linsey Perry, Jon Boggs, and everyone at the University of Tennessee Press expended in bringing this project to fruition. I am grateful to copyeditor Elizabeth Crowder for her careful eye and to Tricia Gesner for her assistance in wrangling photos. Will Coffman and Zack Bray read pieces of the manuscript and indulged my occasional jabbering about it, and Dan Carman, Mark Hoffman, and Walt Robertson kindly served as lunchtime sounding boards. The reference staffs at the Herman B. Wells Library at Indiana University, the William T. Young Library at the University of Kentucky, and the Keeneland Library were knowledgeable and helpful.

On a further saccharine note, I would like to express my appreciation for sportswriters. Even when I knew nothing more about them than their names on a byline, they were some of my first heroes. Today, reading dusty descriptions of games and players from the distant past is one of the pleasures of a project like this.

More specifically, veteran turf writer and editor Ed Bowen was the first journalist I was personally introduced to as a child. Since then, he has been gracious with his time and has provided valuable advice and enjoyable conversation.

Years ago, columnist Mark Story generously supervised a high-school quasi-internship at the *Lexington Herald-Leader*. He introduced a classmate and me to the daily mechanics of sports journalism. That experience was enlightening and instructive. And Jim Miller, a former sportswriter and self-described "old comma cop" (in addition to his various other professional titles and accomplishments), read an early draft of this manuscript and provided expert editorial suggestions.

Finally, among her many contributions to my life, great and small, Maegan took up more than her share of the parenting slack in the course of this project. It would be hard to imagine writing this book, let alone raising three kids, without her.

1968

Introduction

Amid antiwar protests, political assassinations, and urban unrest, by the summer of 1968 the United States had descended into its most domestically dissonant era since the Civil War. Americans were divided along nearly every demographic line imaginable. The looming presidential election only added urgency to the cultural wars raging on the streets, in newspapers, and at dinner tables. Half a world away, in Vietnam, half a million US servicemen were fighting what was increasingly understood to be an unwinnable war. The conflict had already claimed twenty-five thousand American lives.

The leading presidential candidates were an unusually uninspiring lot, and the ostensible opportunity to exert influence at the voting booths only heightened Americans' collective sense of impotence. Richard Rovere described the situation in *Atlantic Monthly.* "Never in our history has the individual seemed as wretched and despairing as he is today," he wrote, "and seldom have free men anywhere felt so thwarted and powerless in their relations to government democratically chosen. Never have disaffection, alienation, and frustration been more widespread." Pollster George Gallup echoed the sentiments: "All the time we've been operating, 32 years now, I've never known a time like this—when people are so disillusioned and cynical."[1]

With the electoral process failing to provide an adequate outlet for deep political frustrations, other aspects of American life became politicized to an unusual degree. The less powerful used what leverage they had where they could to effect change. People in positions of authority who thought that progressive forces were advancing too swiftly built bulwarks against disruption. In that environment of social turmoil, racial animosity, mass protest, and youthful disenchantment, even sports were contested political terrain.

Sports can lend a façade of stability to an unstable world. But in 1968 they provided further evidence, for those who sought it, that American society was coming unmoored. As shaped and debated by an increasingly politically conscious cadre of sports journalists and pundits, the year's major American sports stories reflected the nation's broader disorder and fomented further rancor: A heavyweight champion waited in sports exile pending his appeal of a conviction for draft evasion. The strict interpretations of an arcane rule cost a jovial foreigner a playoff spot at the Masters golf tournament. A doping scandal rocked the Kentucky Derby. An unorthodox rendition of the national anthem at the World Series elicited outrage from baseball fans across the country. And two sprinters shocked the nation with a silent gesture of protest at the Mexico City Olympics. In molding and reporting these stories, American sportswriters fanned the flames of dissension on both sides of contentious issues.

Of course, there is nothing magical about the turning of a page on a calendar, and any endeavor to neatly cordon off the events of 1968 from their antecedents is necessarily a contrivance. The social, political, and economic environments that produced the upheavals of the late 1960s had centuries-old roots. Urban turbulence, violent repression, political assassinations, and mass protest were hardly novel phenomena. And social discord was not limited to the United States in 1968, when popular uprisings swept across much of the globe, from Paris to Prague to Mexico City. But the events of 1968 have come to symbolize the end of a post–World War II era in the United States defined in part by a widespread faith in American institutions' ability to provide boundless economic prosperity and solve major problems at home and abroad. And in hindsight, that year can be seen as an inflection point in American political history.

The major American news stories of the year—the Tet Offensive in Vietnam, President Johnson's decision not to seek reelection, the assassinations of Martin Luther King Jr. and Robert F. Kennedy, violence at the Democratic National Convention in Chicago, Nixon's election—form a convenient narrative arc of their own. But they also provide context for another story in which sport transcended its traditional role as a distraction from the complexities of daily existence and became a part of the complexities. Otherwise trivial games entered the realm of serious public discourse to an unprecedented extent. From that crucible of quarrels a new sports landscape would ultimately emerge, one in which pro football ascended to American sports supremacy and professional athletes acquired a modicum of increased autonomy with the advent of free agency. Two of the outstanding athletes of 1968—a Super Bowl champion antihero quarterback and a maligned World Series scapegoat—would catalyze those developments.

While sports had never been given more serious shrift, 1968 was certainly not the first time that they had converged with politics in America. Power and politics have been inescapably intertwined with American sports since the colonial era. Many ubiquitous political terms and metaphors, including "dark horse" candidate, "running mate," and even the notion of an election as a "race," have nineteenth-century sporting roots. Less abstractly, African American jockeys who dominated Thoroughbred racing for much of the nineteenth century were chased out of the sport by white owners, trainers, and riders by the early 1900s. These equestrians had achieved a level of success that threatened traditional racial, social, and economic order in America. Boxer Jack Johnson's knockout of Jim Jeffries in Reno, Nevada, on July 4, 1910, caused nationwide riots that resulted in hundreds of injuries and arrests, and perhaps as many as two dozen deaths. Later, Johnson fled the country to escape trumped-up criminal charges related to his relationship with a white woman.

Jesse Owens's performance at the 1936 Berlin Olympic Games struck a symbolic blow for democracy against Adolph Hitler's Nazi regime. That fall, Owens campaigned on behalf of Republican presidential nominee Alf Landon, making political hay of what he felt was a snub from Franklin Roosevelt. The president had failed to send a note of congratulations or issue a White House invitation to the winner of four gold medals. Two years later, Joe Louis's rematch knockout of German heavyweight champion Max Schmeling made the "Brown Bomber" one of the first African American national celebrities. And Jackie Robinson integrated Major League Baseball in 1947, years before federal legislation would require the same of hotels and restaurants.

More recently, the presidential election of 2016 served as a backdrop to national controversy when San Francisco 49ers quarterback Colin Kaepernick first declined to stand during the ritual performance of the national anthem at an NFL exhibition game. When asked about the gesture, Kaepernick, a biracial son of white adoptive parents, explained that he intended to draw attention to police brutality and social injustice in the United States. But he also drew the ire of presidential candidate Donald Trump. "Maybe he should find a country that works better for him," Trump told a radio host.[2]

As Kaepernick continued his pregame protests that season, public reaction was sharply divided. Brian T. Smith's column in the *Houston Chronicle* typified much of the passionate criticism of the quarterback. "I guess no one bothered to tell the guy who went 2-for-6 for 14 yards that the country he's protesting has had an African-American as its publicly elected president the last eight years," Smith wrote. "America allows Kaepernick to make a base salary of $11.9 million by sitting on the bench and failing to deliver on his athletic promise. The safety our flag provides also gives Kaepernick the right to defy it. The freedom so many have died for and will continue to sacrifice their lives for—the America Kaepernick so ignorantly takes for granted—allows him to be an idiot in the USA."[3]

The following year, the twenty-nine-year-old Kaepernick, who had led the 49ers to the Super Bowl during the 2012 season, was unable to find a team with a roster spot available to him. In Kaepernick's absence during the 2017 season, some two hundred NFL players kneeled or raised a fist during the anthem, and athletes in other sports made gestures of solidarity with the movement he had started. President Trump called on NFL teams to punish the protesters. "Wouldn't you love to see one of these NFL owners, when somebody disrespects our flag, to say, 'Get that son of a bitch off the field right now,'" he yelled at a rally in Alabama. Vice President Mike Pence left an Indianapolis Colts game in feigned bewilderment after a group of players took a knee during the pregame hymn. "President Trump and I will not dignify any event that disrespects our soldiers, our Flag, or our National Anthem," Pence explained.[4]

The Trump administration's condemnation of the protesting athletes resonated with political supporters. But this position was incongruous with a statement Trump issued upon the 2016 death of the most famous American athlete and dissident of the 1960s. "Muhammad Ali is dead at 74!" Trump tweeted. "A truly great champion and a wonderful guy. He will be missed by all!" By the time of his death, Ali had become nearly universally beloved. But in 1968, exiled from boxing while appealing a conviction for refusing military induction, he had been the most divisive figure in American sports, and arguably the most polarizing person in the entire nation.[5]

Amid all the acrimony that year, facially frivolous sports provided a platform for dissent and a venue for serious ideological debate in the United States. And in this current historical moment when daily news cycles amplify American political animus, the echoes of the past reverberating through the nation's cultural wars bring a heightened relevance to the events of a half century ago. Sports mattered in that pivotal and iconic year. And they continue to matter today, when sports controversies, both historic and contemporary, provide instructive glimpses into the nature of persistent division in the United States.

Prologue

December 31, 1967

It was the coldest New Year's Eve on record in Green Bay, Wisconsin, but fans filled the stands at Lambeau Field to watch their Packers play the Dallas Cowboys for the NFL championship. The game, known to history as the Ice Bowl, would be remembered as one of the greatest in the history of American football. In the aftermath of pregame warm-ups, the field was visibly mangled, and parts were frozen solid. The temperature at kickoff was minus thirteen degrees Fahrenheit, with wind chills reaching an estimated forty-six degrees below zero.

The steam radiating from the crowd was unlike anything the Packers' public-address announcer had seen. "There was this incredible haze of breath, tens of thousands of puffs coming out," he recalled. "Like seeing big buffaloes in an enormous herd on the winter plains. It was prehistoric." Packers defensive leader Ray Nitschke, who had lost his four front teeth playing without a facemask in college, recalled that the home team was not fazed by the weather. "The elements? That's all part of the mental toughness that Lombardi always talked about. When you go out there, you go out there with the idea of winning. We knew we were kind of at the end."[1]

The arctic setting gives the surviving NFL Films game footage the appearance of emanating from an ancient era, a fitting record of the swan song of head coach Vince Lombardi. He had been hinting at retirement and would, in fact, step away from the Green Bay sideline at the end of the season. Bill Russell, the player-coach of another of the fading American sports dynasties of the era, once noted that Lombardi "was much more of a celebrity across the country than any of his players–in fact, more than anybody who'd ever played pro football." Both Lombardi and his team seemed to be holdovers from football's past. Green Bay was the last small-market team in big-time American sports, a link to the founding generation of professional football.[2]

After surrendering two early touchdowns, the Cowboys' "Doomsday" defense shut down the Packers for much of the second half. Green Bay trailed 17-14 when they took possession at their own thirty-two with less than five minutes to play. Quarterback Bart Starr led a disciplined drive that stalled two feet from the Dallas goal line, where Green Bay called its final time-out with sixteen seconds remaining, facing third and goal. Starr ran to the sideline to discuss the situation with Lombardi, who told him, "Run it! And let's get the hell out of here." Back in the huddle, Starr called a play for fullback Chuck Mercein, but he had no intention of risking a fumbled handoff. When the center snapped the ball, Starr kept it, plunging into the end zone behind All-Pro guard Jerry Kramer's block for the winning score. The Packers secured a still-unmatched third consecutive NFL title.

Two weeks later, Green Bay would anticlimactically trample the over-matched Oakland Raiders in the second AFL-NFL World Championship Game. But in the locker room after their Ice Bowl triumph, some Packers players were already in a nostalgic mood, sensing they were approaching the end of an unprecedented run of success. "There is a great deal of love for one another on this club. Perhaps we're living in Camelot," Kramer said, refer-encing the Arthurian legend—a time and place that never really was—that Jackie Kennedy had wistfully attached to the memory of the John F. Kennedy White House after her husband's assassination.[3]

Green Bay fans *brave brutally cold conditions at the 1967 NFL Championship Game against the Dallas Cowboys, known to posterity as the Ice Bowl. The Packers' win gave coach Vince Lombardi a since-unmatched third consecutive league title in his final year on the Green Bay sidelines. (AP Photo/File)*

one
Leap Year

In some cultures, the arrival of leap year is a portent of doom. The first hundred days of 1968 in the United States provided plenty of evidence for anyone inclined to endorse such a superstition. In his State of the Union address on January 17, President Lyndon Johnson acknowledged, "Our country is challenged, at home and abroad." Since his last annual report to Congress, the US military had become further enmeshed in the war in Vietnam, and mass protests and deadly urban riots had rocked the home front. The previous year had been a difficult one for the president and for the nation. But 1968 would be worse.

On January 23, North Korean patrol boats captured the American spy ship USS *Pueblo*. One of the eighty-three Americans aboard the ship was killed, and the rest were captured, interrogated, and held as prisoners of war. Though American officials maintained the *Pueblo* had been in international water, the North Koreans insisted that it had violated the communist country's territorial sovereignty. The Johnson administration faced criticism both for its soft response to the seizure and for finding itself in the quandary in the first place. On the Senate floor, South Dakota Republican Karl E. Mundt demanded a congressional investigation to determine "who [was] responsible for this episode," which he labeled "a shocking, reckless and needless adventure in this area, imperiling both the peace and prestige of the United States."[1]

A week after the *Pueblo* was captured, North Vietnamese and Viet Cong forces launched a series of surprise attacks on cities across South Vietnam. Shortly after midnight on January 30, during the Vietnamese lunar New Year holiday, these troops caught the American and South Vietnamese militaries unprepared for what would later be called the Tet Offensive. Particularly unnerving to Americans was the news that nineteen Viet Cong warriors in a truck and a taxicab had briefly breached security lines at the US embassy compound in Saigon. The attack left one marine guard and seven military police dead. The Tet Offensive dealt a serious blow to American morale; many questioned for the first time whether the United States was in fact winning the war as they had been led to believe.

American officials did their best to put a positive spin on the news. The commander of US forces in Vietnam, Gen. William Westmoreland, said that he had "the enemy on the run." And National Security Advisor Walt Whitman Rostow called the attack "the greatest blunder of Ho Chi Minh's career." But a growing number of Americans began to suspect that the situation in Vietnam was more complicated. The confusion was understandable in light of statements like that from an American officer responding to a question about hundreds of charred bodies near a provincial capital: "It became necessary to destroy the town to save it."[2]

Some American political leaders had already concluded that President Johnson's war policies were not working. In an address to an assembly of authors in Chicago, Sen. Robert Kennedy declared, "Our enemy, savagely striking at will across all of South Vietnam, has finally shattered the mask of official illusion from which we have concealed our true circumstances even from ourselves. . . . We have misconceived the nature of the war. We have sought to resolve by military might a conflict whose issue depends upon the will and conviction of the South Vietnamese people. It is like sending a lion to halt an epidemic of jungle rot." He concluded by suggesting, "[The Johnson administration should] face the reality that a military victory is not in sight and that it probably will never come."[3]

An image that appeared alongside reports of the Tet Offensive in American newspapers provided shocking visual accompaniment to the disturbing descriptions of the struggle. Associated Press photographer Eddie Adams would

South Vietnamese Gen. Nguyen Ngoc Loan, chief of the National Police, executed a suspected Viet Cong officer in a Saigon street. The image gave American newspaper readers a graphic introduction to the brutality of the war in Vietnam. (AP Photos/Eddie Adams, File)

win a Pulitzer Prize for his photo of South Vietnamese national police chief Gen. Nguyen Ngoc Loan firing a bullet into the head of a Viet Cong prisoner on a Saigon street. The same day, many US newspapers reported Richard Milhous Nixon's official entry into the Republican presidential primary. Nixon had served two terms as Dwight Eisenhower's vice president but had faced a steep path back from the political wastelands after his narrow loss to John F. Kennedy in the 1960 presidential election and subsequent loss in the California gubernatorial race two years later. The crestfallen candidate had punctuated the latter defeat with a sour-grapes press conference in which he told reporters, "You won't have Nixon to kick around any more because, gentlemen, this is my last press conference."[4]

"It had seemed the absolute end of a career," wrote journalist and novelist Norman Mailer. "Self-pity in public was as irreversible as suicide." But Nixon did eventually recover, moving to New York to take a job with a top Wall Street law firm. There, he had a chance to ingratiate himself to the "eastern establishment" and build a foundation for a political rebirth. Nixon surrounded himself with a new set of advisors and supporters and began to reshape his tarnished public image. Members of his new team included speechwriter Patrick Buchanan, economic advisor Alan Greenspan, and television wunderkind Roger Ailes, who would later become the founding CEO of Fox News.[5]

Nixon met twenty-eight-year-old Ailes during a 1967 appearance on the *Mike Douglas Show* and lamented to the young producer, "It's a shame a man has to use gimmicks like this to get elected."

"Television is not a gimmick," Ailes told the candidate.

Nixon was impressed with the young man and hired him to produce a series of infomercial-type television programs. During each one, Nixon would field questions from a handpicked panel of supporters in a faux–town hall setting. These sessions reintroduced a humanized Nixon to voters and helped to remove the taint of defeat from him. Though Nixon promised to "end the war and win the peace" in Vietnam, he gave little indication of how he planned to accomplish the former or what the latter even meant.[6]

The week after Nixon's announcement, former Alabama governor George "Segregation Forever" Wallace officially joined the presidential race as a third-party candidate, declaring, "So-called civil rights laws are really an attack on the property rights of this country and on the free enterprise system and local government . . . and I would try to have them changed in Congress." When he had first run for governor, in 1958, Wallace had been racially progressive by local standards. In fact, the NAACP had endorsed him. But when he lost to an unabashed segregationist, he attributed the defeat to his opponent's race-baiting and support from the Ku Klux Klan. "Well, boys," Wallace told his aides, "no other son-of-a-bitch will ever out-nigger me again." He stayed true to his pledge, making a national name for himself in 1963 by standing in a doorway to prevent two African American students from registering for classes at the University of Alabama.[7]

As a presidential candidate in 1968, Wallace promised to end the antiwar protests that seemed to be growing in strength and number each month. "When we get to be President, and some anarchist lies down in front of our car, it'll be the last car he'll ever lie down in front of," Wallace promised. The base of his support was clearly in the South, but he tried to find common ground with whites of all regions. "People always say that George Wallace just appeals to the crackers, the peckerwoods, and the rednecks," he was fond of saying, unafraid to speak in the third person. "Well, George Wallace says

Governor George Wallace *stood defiantly in the door of the Foster Auditorium at the University of Alabama in an attempt to prevent the racial integration of the school on June 11, 1963. (Library of Congress, Photo by Warren K. Leffler)*

there's an awful lot of rednecks in this country—and they're not all in the South!" Wallace ridiculed what he called "the bearded professor who thinks he knows how to settle the Vietnam War when he hasn't got enough sense to park his bicycle straight." The candidate also received an early endorsement from the national president of the Fraternal Order of Police, who said of civil rights protesters, "We are at war with an enemy just as dangerous as the Viet Cong." Wallace courted fans of strict law enforcement, saying, "I'd let the police run this country for a couple of years. I'm not talking about a police state, but sometimes it takes a police state to run some people."[8]

In a year of unusual news stories, perhaps no dispatch was more shocking than that delivered by Walter Cronkite, the CBS anchor who had introduced the half-hour television news format in the fall of 1963. His sign-off line—"And that's the way it is"—said plenty about the nature of news in that era and underscored Cronkite's stature within that system. On February 27, 1968, Cronkite presented prime-time audiences his observations concerning a recent trip to Vietnam. "To say that we are closer to victory today is to believe, in the face of the evidence, the optimists who have been wrong in the past," he reported. "To suggest we are on the edge of defeat is to yield to unreasonable pessimism. To say that we are mired in stalemate seems the only realistic, yet unsatisfactory, conclusion."[9]

The degree to which Cronkite's report influenced public opinion or public policy has been debated. But for a nation that prided itself on never having lost a war, his decision to enter the editorial realm was at the very least a harbinger of crumbling confidence in President Lyndon Johnson's strategy in Vietnam. In the coming weeks, as General Westmoreland requested two hundred thousand additional troops for the war effort, NBC News aired a special that concluded, "The war, as the administration has defined it, is being lost. Laying aside all other arguments, the time is at hand when we must decide whether it is futile to destroy Vietnam in the effort to save it." *Newsweek* shared similar sentiments: "Unless it is prepared to indulge in the ultimate, horrifying escalation—the use of nuclear weapons—it now appears that the U.S. must accept the fact that it will never be able to achieve decisive military superiority in Vietnam."[10]

Sen. Eugene McCarthy, a long shot presidential candidate from Minnesota, attempted to capitalize on a surge of antiwar sentiment. He also hoped to convince the Democratic Party to adopt an antiwar platform plank at its August convention. McCarthy plowed much of his modest campaign coffers into New Hampshire, site of the first Democratic primary of the season. An enthusiastic team of young New Englanders supported the senator, who was a devout Catholic, a poet, and the son of a farmer. He had been a collegiate baseball and ice hockey star before teaching high school after graduation, and he later became chair of the Sociology Department at the College of St. Thomas in Minnesota. Political journalist Nick Thimmesch called him "a quiet, witty man of gray presence." And the *New York Times* described him as a "political scholar-gypsy" who would drop into committee hearings then leave in boredom, "retiring to his office, where visitors [might] find him reading Yeats rather than the Congressional Record."[11]

McCarthy said that he first began to consider a remote chance of victory against the incumbent president when he "realized that you could go into any bar in the country and insult Johnson and nobody would punch you in the nose." Hundreds of young supporters cut their hair and shaved their beards to go "clean for Gene," but even the candidate himself acknowledged that he faced seriously long odds. Nevertheless, he felt a moral obligation to give a voice to the growing number of Americans expressing serious concern with

US military policy in Vietnam and he hoped to appeal to a "constituency of conscience."[12]

Winning in New Hampshire initially appeared to be an impossibly tall order. The Democrats there tended to be hawkish, and the economy was humming with a vibrant electronics industry fueled by Defense Department contracts. Polls showed McCarthy losing 71–18 only weeks before the primary, but on Election Day he took 42 percent of the popular vote and 20 of 24 delegates. *Newsweek* called his performance an "astonishing political upset," declaring, "In the space of five days last week, a phenomenon that began as little more than a courageous exercise in political dissent was transformed into a convulsion that shook every corner of the American political landscape." In 1968, state primaries were still much less significant in determining presidential nominees than they would soon become. Most states did not even hold primaries, and many of the states that did held nonbinding ones. Party bosses wielded significant power over state delegates and nominating conventions. But if a candidate could build momentum during the primaries, demonstrating broad popular appeal and electability, it was theoretically possible for primary results to influence party politics on a national scale.[13]

Convinced that Johnson could be defeated, Bobby Kennedy announced his candidacy later that week in the same Senate Caucus Room where his brother had declared his intent to run in 1960. "I do not run for the presidency merely to oppose any man, but to propose new policies," Bobby Kennedy said. "I run because I am convinced that this country is on a perilous course and because I have such strong feelings about what must be done, and I feel that I'm obliged to do all I can. I run to seek new policies—policies to end the bloodshed in Vietnam and in our cities, policies to close the gaps that now exist between black and white, between rich and poor, between young and old, in this country and around the rest of the world." He concluded by evoking his brother's New Frontier grandiosity: "I do not lightly dismiss the dangers and the difficulties of challenging an incumbent President. But these are not ordinary times, and this is not an ordinary election. At stake is not simply the leadership of our party or even our country. It is our right to moral leadership of this planet." Sixteen hours before Kennedy invoked American moral authority, it would later be discovered, American soldiers had murdered over five hundred South Vietnamese civilians in what would be known as the My Lai massacre.[14]

Kennedy alienated Democratic Party stalwarts early in the race; he would not promise to support Johnson if the president won the nomination. "I'm loyal to the Democratic Party," Kennedy said, "but I feel stronger about the United States and mankind generally." With an approval rating of 36 percent,

Lyndon B. Johnson *signing the Civil Rights Act of 1968. In the face of declining national popularity, President Lyndon Johnson, announced that he would not run for reelection in 1968. (Library of Congress, Photo by Warren K. Leffler)*

the president faced escalating criticism from both hawks and doves that left only a quarter of Americans believing he was handling the war effort effectively. Kennedy's "grave reservations" about Johnson's candidacy would soon become moot, however.

Johnson addressed a prime-time television audience on March 31, advocating a partial bombing halt in Vietnam, modest troop increases, heavier reliance on the South Vietnam military, and a tax hike to pay for the rising costs of the war. He acknowledged the division and divisiveness within American society, then he issued a stunning declaration: "I shall not seek, and I will not accept, the nomination of my party for another term as your president. . . . With American sons in the field far away, with the American future under challenge right here at home, with our hopes and the world's hopes for peace in the balance every day, I do not believe that I should devote an hour or a day of my time to any personal partisan causes or to any duties other than the awesome duties of this office, the Presidency of your country."[15]

Johnson had spent serious political capital in pursuing his Great Society domestic agenda, including civil rights legislation and antipoverty measures.

After assuming the presidency upon John Kennedy's death in 1963, he had won the 1964 election by one of the largest margins in American history, riding a wave of unprecedented economic prosperity. But by the spring of 1968 America had changed, and voters were ready for a new political direction.

As Johnson later told biographer Doris Kearns Goodwin, "I was being forced over the edge by rioting blacks, demonstrating students, marching welfare mothers, squawking professors, and hysterical reporters. And then the final straw. The thing I feared from the first day of my Presidency was actually coming true. Robert Kennedy had openly announced his intention to reclaim the throne in the memory of his brother. And the American people, swayed by the magic of the name, were dancing in the streets. The whole situation was unbearable for me. After thirty-seven years of public service, I deserved something more than being left alone in the middle of the plain, chased by stampedes on every side."[16]

Johnson's abdication gave some very short-lived optimism to Americans anxious for a new national direction.

——————————

Martin Luther King Jr., the de facto leader of the American civil rights movement for more than a decade, addressed a rally for the Poor People's Campaign on March 23 at Beulah Baptist Church in Augusta, Georgia. "This country has lost its sense of direction, its sense of purpose, and it needs to rearrange its priorities," he told the audience. "For we cannot fight an immoral war in Vietnam where many of our young men are dying and at the same time finance the war on poverty to help our people in this country—white and black people living in what seems like hopeless conditions."[17]

A week later, at a press conference that followed an address at Washington National Cathedral, King said, "I don't like to predict violence, but if nothing is done between now and June to raise ghetto hope, I feel that this summer will not only be as bad but worse than last year." In 1967, dozens were killed and thousands wounded in widespread rioting in urban ghettos across America, most notably Detroit and Newark. The Kerner Commission, established by President Johnson to assess the causes of the rioting, had recently issued its report, which concluded: "[The United States is] moving toward two societies, one black, one white—separate and unequal. . . . Segregation and poverty have created in the racial ghetto a destructive environment totally unknown to most white Americans. . . . What white Americans have never understood—but what the Negro can never forget—is that white society is deeply implicated in the ghetto. White institutions created it, white institutions maintain it, and white society condones it."[18]

The thirty-nine-year-old King gave what would be his final public speech on April 3 at Mason Temple in Memphis, Tennessee, where he was lending support to a sanitation workers' strike for a wage increase and safer working conditions. The walkout occurred after a garbage compactor fatally crushed two workers. It was a stormy night, and King was initially inclined to stay in his motel room, believing that no one would be coming out in such foul weather. But he hurried over when his handlers reported that an overflow crowd was waiting for him at the church. Addressing threats on his body and his life, King declared: "I don't know what will happen now. We've got some difficult days ahead. But it really doesn't matter with me now, because I've been to the mountaintop. And I don't mind. Like anybody, I would like to live a long life; longevity has its place. But I'm not concerned about that now. I just want to do God's will. And He's allowed me to go up to the mountain. And I've looked over. And I've seen the Promised Land. I may not get there with you. But I want you to know tonight that we, as a people, will get to the Promised Land. And so, I'm happy tonight. I'm not worried about anything. I'm not fearing any man. Mine eyes have seen the glory of the coming of the Lord."[19]

Less than twenty-four hours later, King was fatally shot as he stood on the balcony at the Lorraine Motel, speaking with friends before a dinner engagement. The assassin, James Earl Ray, had grown up impoverished in small Illinois and Missouri towns along the Mississippi River. He and his seven siblings were abandoned by his father, removed from his alcoholic mother's custody, and placed in foster care. After being kicked out of the military, Ray began a professional life of crime, serving stints in prison for armed robbery and burglary. Since his 1967 escape from the Missouri State Penitentiary, where inmates had widely discussed the possibility of a $50,000 bounty on Dr. King's head, Ray had been on the lam and had developed an interest in the George Wallace presidential campaign.

As news of King's death spread, violence was reported in at least 140 American cities, including widespread disturbances in more than three dozen. In Washington, DC, deadly rioting reflected many African Americans' deep frustration with poor living conditions, high unemployment, mistreatment by police, and underperforming schools. Twelve people were killed in six days of fire and disorder there. Army troops surrounded the White House, and marines manned machine guns on the Capitol steps. In Chicago, Mayor Richard J. Daley gave police orders to "shoot to kill" arsonists and "shoot to maim" looters. Stokely Carmichael, the revolutionary civil rights activist and

In the wake of Martin Luther King's assassination, *violent riots swept through more than 100 major US cities. Some of the worst destruction occurred in Washington DC, where soldiers pictured here protected the Capitol.*

More than 1,000 buildings were burned in Washington DC during five days of rioting. (Library of Congress)

Black Power advocate, told shocked supporters in King's Southern Christian Leadership Conference office in Washington, "Now that they've taken Dr. King off, it's time to end this nonviolence bullshit." Once the nation's major urban areas calmed, dozens had been killed, 2,500 had been injured, and hundreds of buildings had been burned, causing millions of dollars in property damage. Police had made 20,000 arrests, and 65,000 National Guardsmen had seen riot duty in the worst American domestic disturbance since the Civil War.[20]

The *Chicago Tribune* editorial board reacted to the riots and to what its members considered a timid response from law enforcement: "The rioters here have taken advantage of the wave of sentimentality and assumed guilt that has swept the country because a single individual, presumably demented, gunned down the Rev. Martin Luther King. . . . The lesson of all recent riots has been that when public officials and the public at large lean over backwards in an attempt to appease the lawbreakers cities are in deep trouble." The board concluded its editorial by warning Mayor Daley not to "fall into the same category as spineless and indecisive mayors who muffed early riot control in such cities as Los Angeles and Newark." Daley would make sure he did not fall into any such category when the Democratic National Convention came to his town that August.[21]

Indianapolis remained conspicuously peaceful in the aftermath of King's death. When news of the assassination broke, Robert Kennedy was on his way to deliver a campaign speech there, in the heart of the blighted inner city. Though police warned him that they could not guarantee his safety, Kennedy declined to cancel his appearance. From the back of a flatbed truck he gave a moving speech in which he confirmed that King had died, and asked the large crowd not to express their anger and dismay through violence. He alluded to his brother's death for the first time in public and quoted his favorite Greek poet. Then he said, "What we need in the United States is not division; what we need in the United States is not hatred; what we need in the United States is not violence and lawlessness, but is love, and wisdom, and compassion toward one another, and a feeling of justice toward those who still suffer within our country, whether they be white or whether they be black." Kennedy concluded, "Let's dedicate ourselves to what the Greeks wrote so many years ago: to tame the savageness of man and make gentle the life of this world. Let us dedicate ourselves to that, and say a prayer for our country and for our people. Thank you very much."[22]

One audience member later recalled, "We went there for trouble [but] after he spoke we couldn't get nowhere." Another said, "The black power guys didn't get no place after the man speak."[23]

After fiery riots in Boston on Thursday night, James Brown, the self-styled Godfather of Soul, was scheduled to perform in Boston Garden on Friday. At the behest of city officials who hoped to keep people in their homes, Boston PBS affiliate WGBH televised the show live, and then rebroadcast it at 2:00 a.m. The presenter introducing the program might not have been familiar with the popular act, referring to "Negro singer Jimmy Brown and his group." Brown urged his audience to remain calm. "Let's not do anything to dishonor Dr. King," he said. "Stay home. You kids especially." Given the deep-seated racial tension in Boston, it was a testament to Brown's musicianship and star power that the highly segregated city reported less crime that night than it would expect on a typical Friday in April.[24]

That same night, the Boston Celtics and Philadelphia 76ers were scheduled to begin their Eastern Division playoff series in Philadelphia. Led by 7'1" superstar Wilt Chamberlain, Philadelphia had defeated Boston the previous year on its way to the NBA championship, raising speculation that Boston's unprecedented period of domination was over. When Philadelphia finished eight games ahead of Boston in the regular season, chants of "Boston's dead" could be heard at 76er games. But Boston had beaten Detroit in six games in the division semifinals to set up a showdown with the Sixers.

Celtics player-coach Bill Russell had participated in King's March on Washington and was a steadfast civil rights supporter. His mind was fixed on the news from Memphis, and he "was in a state of shock." After a sleepless night, Russell, along with Chamberlin, was inclined to postpone the game. But the men also worried that a late cancellation would precipitate a violent reaction from angry fans. Russell had won two NCAA championships at the University of San Francisco, an Olympic gold medal, and five NBA MVP Awards. *Sports Illustrated* would name him Sportsman of the Year in 1968. The following spring, he would add an eleventh NBA championship to his long list of accomplishments in his final professional season, capping an incomparable career and closing a dynastic era for the winningest team in the history of the sport. The year after Russell's retirement, the franchise would endure its first losing season in two decades. Yet despite all his triumphs in Boston, the fans there never fully embraced him.[25]

Once, after a weekend away, Russell had returned to his home outside Boston to find that vandals had defaced it, spray-painting "NIGGA" on a wall and defecating in his bed. The Celtics were the first in the NBA to draft an African American player and the first to play five black players at the same time. They became the first to hire a head coach of color when Russell was named player-coach in 1966, replacing the legendary Red Auerbach. They were among the most racially progressive sports franchises in America during the fifties and sixties, and, perhaps not coincidentally, the team bordered on unprofitability due to low attendance.[26]

When players for both the Celtics and 76ers met to discuss postponing the playoff game in the wake of King's murder, tensions ran high. Celtics forward Bailey Howell, a white southerner, added to the strain by arguing that the game should be played because King had no official title that would justify a cancellation in his honor. The teams ultimately agreed to play, and Boston won by nine. After a postponement of Game Two for a national day of mourning ordered by President Johnson, the 76ers took three straight to move within one win of the finals. No NBA team had ever climbed from that hole to win a seven-game series. But Boston won the final three games against Philadelphia before beating the Los Angeles Lakers in six to capture their tenth title in twelve years.

The Major League Baseball season had been scheduled to start the day before King's funeral, and Commissioner William "Spike" Eckert, who had risen to the rank of lieutenant general in three decades of Air Force service, initially left the decision of whether to play ball up to the team owners. The Pittsburgh Pirates were to open the season in Houston, and the Astros had declared that the game would proceed as planned. But the Pirates players, led by star right fielder Roberto Clemente, refused to play. As Clemente later recalled, "When Martin Luther King died, they come and ask the Negro players if we should play. I say, 'If you have to ask Negro players, then we do not have a great country.'" St. Louis Cardinals star pitcher Bob Gibson later wrote, "I reeled from the impact of the assassination—the cold-blooded murder of the one man in my lifetime who had been able to capture the public's attention about racial injustice, break through some of the age-old social barriers and raise the spirits and hopes of black people across the country." [27]

Gibson's teammate, catcher Tim McCarver, recalled the pitcher's response to news of King's death:

Everybody on the club was dismayed by what happened to Martin Luther King. It was a very disorienting time in many respects and that was probably the hardest moment. Bob and I had a very serious discussion in the clubhouse that morning. He was very emotional and initially he turned his back on me.

Probably the last person he wanted to talk to that morning was a white man from Memphis, of all places. But I confronted him on that, as I knew he would have done if the tables had been turned. I told him that I had grown up in an environment of severe prejudice, but if I were any indication, it was possible for people to change their attitudes.

He didn't really want to be calmed down and told me in so many words that it was plainly impossible for a white man to completely overcome prejudice. . . . I found myself in the unfamiliar position of arguing that the races were equal and that we were all the same. It was a soul-searching type of thing and I believe Bob and I reached a meeting of the minds that morning. That was the kind of talk we often had on the Cardinals. [28]

Once it became clear that substantial numbers of players intended to sit out any game played the day of King's funeral, Commissioner Eckert pushed back the start of the season until the day after the memorial services. At DC Stadium, home of the Washington Senators, Vice President Hubert Horatio

Humphrey threw out the ceremonial first pitch. The stadium, which would be renamed for Robert F. Kennedy the following year, was adorned with patriotic red, white, and blue bunting for the occasion, but the vice president's favorite team, the Minnesota Twins, shut out the perennial losers. Bob Addie, who covered the Senators for the *Washington Post*, wrote that the return of baseball afforded Americans the chance to "get back to the ordinary things in life" and provided "a touch of normalcy" for the chaotic times. But the ten thousand empty seats at the nominally sold-out stadium belied the notion that any normalcy had returned to the nation's capital. Soldiers guarded the stadium grounds, which had been used as a staging area and camp for troops patrolling the riotous DC streets that week.[29]

King's death had stunned the nation, but politicians and editorialists soon capitalized on the opportunity to make points about the ills of society. California governor Ronald Reagan called the murder "a great tragedy that began when we began compromising with law and order, and people started choosing which laws they'd break."[30] And on the morning of King's funeral, the *Chicago Tribune* published a lengthy editorial capturing some of the political and cultural acrimony of the era:

> A day of mourning is in order, if not particularly for Dr. King. This country should repent its ways. It should mourn for its fall from grace. It should look into its heart and abjure the evils to which it has succumbed. . . .
>
> Look about you. Moral values are at the lowest level since the decadence of Rome. . . . Drug addiction among the youth is so widespread that we are treated to the spectacle at great universities of faculty-student committees solemnly decreeing that this is no longer a matter for correction under law. At countless universities, the doors of dormitories are open to mixed company with no supervision.
>
> Dress is immodest. Pornography floods the newsstands and bookstores. . . . Students terrorize faculties and university presidents and assert that they should govern the administration and dictate the curriculum. We are knee-deep in hippies, marijuana, LSD, and the other hallucinogens. . . .
>
> We have spawned a generation raised on the maxims of Baby Doctor Spock that permissiveness is beautiful. If the brat squawks loud and long enough, you cure him by giving him anything he wants. The same rule has been meekly adopted as a panacea for racial tension. If you are black, so goes the contention, you are right, and you must be indulged in every wish. Why, sure, break the window and make off with the color TV set, the case of liquor, the beer, the dress, the coat, and the shoes. We won't shoot you. That would be "police brutality."

So goes the fashionable "liberal" reasoning of the day. And the corollary is: If you are white, you are wrong. Feel guilty about it. Assume the collective guilt of all your progenitors, even if neither you nor anyone you know is a descendant of slave owners. Yield the sidewalk to the migrants from the south who have descended on your cities. Honor their every want, because the "liberals" tell you that it is your fault that they have not educated themselves, developed responsibility, trained themselves to hold jobs, or are shiftless and dependent on your taxes. . . .

This country will turn to a party and to a man who resolutely stand up to the fomenters of strife and say, "This far and no farther." Yes, this nation and people need a day of mourning—a day in which they look into their hearts, take stock of their conscience, and decide whether repentance is to be their salvation—if any is to be had."[31]

That morning, friends, family, and dignitaries gathered at Atlanta's Ebenezer Baptist Church for King's funeral service. A good portion of the sanctuary's 750 seats were reserved for white politicians, none of whom was from the South. Dozens of congressmen and senators were present, including Vice President Humphrey, Bobby Kennedy, and Richard Nixon. Nixon had demanded "swift and sure retaliation" against the rioters in the aftermath of King's death, and the candidate's regional campaign director had to apologize to southern Republican leaders for his attendance at the funeral.[32]

Some of the nation's most famous athletes, including Jackie Robinson, Bill Russell, and Wilt Chamberlain, joined the political contingent. After the service 100,000 people lined the streets as a mule team pulled a farm wagon bearing King's casket through downtown Atlanta to the campus of Morehouse College, where a larger public ceremony would be held. President Johnson did not come to Atlanta, citing safety concerns.

Georgia governor Lester Maddox was also not in attendance. He had first come to national attention in 1964, when he had refused to serve three black Georgia Tech students at his Atlanta restaurant, calling them "no good dirty devils" and "dirty communists." Maddox then sold his restaurant in protest of the 1964 Civil Rights Act and erected a monument in front of the building decrying the "death of private property rights in America." Holed up in his office after refusing to allow a state funeral for King, whom he considered "an enemy of our country," Maddox assembled a team of state troopers at the capitol to ensure order. The governor promised that if anyone tried to storm the building, he would "shoot them down and stack them up."[33]

Some of the most prominent and influential athletes and entertainers in America had attended King's funeral, but the most famous one was not among them. Muhammad Ali had found common ground with King in opposition to the war in Vietnam, and their paths had crossed in the spring of 1967 in Louisville, where the pair had an amiable discussion while King was in town for an SCLC meeting. But Ali rejected King's vision of a racially integrated America and even expressed support for George Wallace's segregationist rhetoric. "Governor Wallace, he tells the truth," Ali told the *Boston Globe*'s Bud Collins in an interview that aired on public television stations across the country. "I don't believe in everything nobody says, but I like when he says Negroes shouldn't push to get into a white neighborhood. . . . If I don't want you, why do you push yourself on me?"[34]

Despite claiming conscientious objector status, Ali had been convicted of draft evasion and sentenced to five years in prison for refusing induction into the armed services. He was free on bail pending appeal in the spring of 1968, but he had been summarily stripped of his boxing titles. Some questioned the sincerity of Ali's conscientious objector claims, but his willingness to sacrifice his livelihood and face prison rather than serve in the military made him a hero to opponents of the Vietnam War. Still, Ali's loudmouth persona and increasingly politicized posture turned off millions of Americans. Even during his absence from the prize ring, no American athlete in that historically divisive era was more visible or more polarizing. No one better exposed the gaping cultural divide in the United States than Muhammad Ali.

As he awaited a decision from the US Court of Appeals for the Fifth Circuit, Ali was stuck in a strange state of limbo. He had been the heavyweight champion of the world and had never lost in a professional prize ring. He was physically willing and able to defend his title, but he was not allowed to fight—every American boxing jurisdiction had banned him. Denied an ability to earn a living in the ring, Ali supported his family as a professional speaker and provocateur, pressing the boundaries of what American society could tolerate from its professional athletes.

Cassius Marcellus Clay Jr. was born in Louisville, Kentucky, in 1942. He would adopt the name Muhammad Ali in 1964 after winning the heavyweight championship, but the name given to him at birth was his father's name, which they shared with the nineteenth-century Kentucky abolitionist. Clay was introduced to boxing at the age of twelve, according to an often-retold story, when his bicycle was stolen. He reported the theft to officer Joe Martin and promised to whup the thief. Martin led a youth boxing program at the Louisville Recreation Department, which he encouraged the boy to join. Clay showed early aptitude and quickly rose through the amateur ranks. He won a gold medal at the 1960 Olympics in Rome and set his sights on the world heavyweight championship.

Most writers bristled at Ali's braggadocio, which defied the unspoken rules of decorum that had long governed the relationship between the sporting press and the people they covered. Yet Muhammad Ali found an ally in an upstart television announcer with an ego at least as large as his own—former attorney Howard Cosell. No relationship would prove more important to Ali's struggle to remain visible in athletic exile than the synergistic one he cultivated with the narcissistic, middle-aged, nasal-voiced broadcaster.

Despite speaking in what has been called "a clutched throat, high-pitched Brooklyn twang with a stately staccato that tended to put equal stress on each syllable of every word, infusing even the most mundane event with high drama," Cosell became the most famous, beloved, and despised sports broadcaster in America. As biographer Dave Kindred notes, "Before Cosell, sports on television was a reverential production. After, it was a circus. He brought to his work a fan's passion, an entertainer's shtick, and (this was new) a journalist's integrity. He had no interest in creating an image of men as heroes simply because they could play a kid's game. Instead, he subjected sports to the examinations Edward R. Murrow and Walter Cronkite made of the day's news." And Cosell found in Ali something of a kindred spirit. "As Ali was the first athlete in the television age to announce his own greatness, Cosell was the first broadcaster," Kindred writes.[35]

Cosell's capacity for self-aggrandizement rubbed plenty of colleagues, critics, and consumers the wrong way. Jim Murray of the *Los Angeles Times* callously called him "the man of a thousand syllables who comes on as if he were reading the tablets of Sinai to a group of retarded children who are hard of hearing and unfamiliar with the language." But Don Ohlmeyer, who worked with Cosell as a producer at ABC Sports, appreciated his historical significance. "Howard was exactly what we all needed at the time," Ohlmeyer said. "The country was going to hell and yet sportswriters had nothing to say about it. They all thought they could just ride it out. But America changed in '68. Sports changed. . . . You couldn't separate sports and society anymore—which was Howard's message all along."[36]

It was a message that would have reached far fewer ears if not for the fighter who called himself "The Greatest." Cosell and Ali formed a formidable

Muhammad Ali stands over Sonny Liston *after a rematch knockout of the former champion in 1965. Ali won the heavyweight title with his first defeat of Liston the previous year, after which Ali announced that he had changed his name from Cassius Clay and declared his affiliation with the Nation of Islam. (AP Photo/John Rooney, File)*

partnership, something akin to a comedy duo, with Cosell content to play the straight man in the many interviews he conducted with Ali on television and radio over the years. Ali's 1964 defeat of the fearsome, heavily favored Sonny Liston to claim the heavyweight title for the first time sent shock waves through the sports world. After the fight, he announced that he had changed his name from Cassius Clay, and he publicly acknowledged his conversion to the Muslim faith and affiliation with the controversial and cultish Nation of Islam, a group that mixed religion and Black Nationalist politics. Millions of American sports fans were appalled.

In February 1966, Ali learned that his draft status had changed from "unfit for military service" to 1-A—available for combat. Before the military lowered its standards in response to the growing need for bodies in Vietnam, Ali had been unable to qualify for the draft due to poor math scores. He told reporters at the time, "When I looked at a lot of them questions, I just didn't know the answers. I didn't even know how to start about finding the answers. I said I was the greatest, not the smartest."[37]

Upon receiving the news of his new draft status, Ali addressed a slew of journalists that had swarmed outside his rented home in North Miami. "I've got a question," he said. "For two years the government caused me international embarrassment, letting people think I was a nut. Sure it bothered me, and my mother and father suffered, and now they jump up and make me 1-A without even an official notification or a test. Why did they let me be considered a nut, an illiterate, for two years? How can they do this without another test to see if I'm any wiser or worser than last time? Why are they so anxious, why are they gunning for me?" The following day a sportswriter from the *Chicago Daily News* asked Ali about the reclassification. "I am a member of the Muslims and we don't go to no wars unless they are declared by Allah himself," Ali said. "I don't have no personal quarrel with those Viet Congs."[38]

Writers lambasted Ali in assorted diatribes, lumping him in with all sorts of ills they saw in American society and culture. The *New York Journal-American*'s Jimmy Cannon sneered, "Clay is part of the Beatle movement. He fits in with the famous singers no one can hear and the punks riding motorcycles with iron crosses pinned to their leather jackets and Batman and the boys with their long dirty hair and the girls with the unwashed look and the college kids dancing naked at secret proms held in apartments and the revolt of students who get a check from dad every first of the month and the painters who copy the labels off soup cans and the surf bums who refuse to work and the whole pampered style-making cult of the bored young." Even the Kentucky Senate took aim at the state's most famous son, passing a resolution stating, "His attitude brings discredit to all loyal Kentuckians and to the names of thousands who gave their lives for this country during his lifetime."[39]

Ali appealed his reclassification to Judge Lawrence Grauman, the hearing officer the Department of Justice appointed to his case, and argued on his own behalf at the hearing: "Sir, I said earlier and I'd like to again make that plain, it would be no trouble for me to go into the Armed Services, [participating in] boxing exhibitions in Vietnam or traveling the country at the expense of the government or living the easy life and not having to get out in the mud and fight and shoot. If it wasn't against my conscience to do it, I would easily do it. I wouldn't raise all this court stuff and I wouldn't go through all of this and lose the millions that I gave up and my image with the American public that I would say is completely dead and ruined because of us in here now." Grauman found that Ali was "not a hypocrite or a faker with reference to his conscientious objector claim."[40]

The US Department of Justice ignored Grauman's nonbinding findings and issued its recommendation to the Louisville draft board that Ali's appeal be denied. Ali was ordered to report for induction, which he intended to refuse. As his induction date neared, Ali continued to share his message with reporters. "Why should they ask me to put on a uniform and go ten thousand miles from home and drop bombs and bullets on brown people in Vietnam while so-called Negro people in Louisville are treated like dogs?" he asked. "If I thought goin' to war would bring freedom and equality to twenty-two million Negroes, they wouldn't have to draft me, I'd join tomorrow. I either have to obey the laws of the land or the laws of Allah. I have nothing to lose by standing up and following my own beliefs. I'll go down in history."[41]

On induction day, Cosell caught up to Ali outside the federal building that housed a US Armed Forces Examining and Entrance Station in Houston, where the boxer had established residence. As Ali headed inside, Cosell asked, "Are you going to take the step, Muhammad?" When he received no answer, Cosell asked again, "Are you going—to take—the step?"

Ali smiled and responded, "Howard Cosell—why don't you take the step."

"I did," Cosell said, "in 1942."[42]

Inside, when the name Cassius Clay was called, Ali did not step forward for induction. An officer warned him that refusal was a criminal act and that he faced a five-year imprisonment and a $10,000 fine. When he again declined to step forward, the officer requested, and Ali produced, a written explanation stating that he claimed an exemption as a minister of Islam.

After the ceremony, outside the federal building, Cosell asked Ali for an interview, but Nation of Islam leader Elijah Muhammad had told Ali to stop speaking to the press. Cosell negotiated a compromise and accompanied Ali back to the fighter's hotel, where Cosell read a statement written by Ali's lawyers: "I strongly object to the fact that so many newspapers have given the American public and the world the impression that I have only two alternatives in taking this stand: Either I go to jail or go in the army. There is another alternative and that alternative is justice. If justice prevails, if my Constitutional rights are upheld, I will be forced to go neither to the army nor jail. In the end, I am confident that justice will come my way, for the truth must eventually prevail."

Ali then assured Cosell he had nothing further to say, adding "[I] may have talked too much."

"If you did, Muhammad, it will be one hell of a scoop," Cosell said.[43]

Later that day, the New York State Athletic Commission suspended Ali's boxing license and withdrew its recognition of him as world heavyweight

Muhammad Ali speaks to Howard Cosell *outside the Armed Forced Induction Center in Houston, Texas, where Ali refused induction into the Army on April 28, 1967, and was subsequently stripped of his boxing titles. Cosell's frequent televised interviews with Ali helped the champion to shape and publicize the persona that would make him the most divisive athlete of his era. (AP Photo)*

champion. Commission chairman Edwin Dooley explained, "[Ali's] refusal to enter the service is regarded by the commission to be detrimental to the best interests of boxing." The other major boxing organizations and jurisdictions soon followed NYSAC's lead in stripping Ali of his title and banning him from fighting.[44] In June 1967, an all-white federal jury needed only twenty-one minutes to convict Ali of draft evasion. Although the US attorney told the court that the government would not object to a lesser punishment, Judge Joe Ingraham imposed the maximum sentence, five years in prison and a $10,000 fine, and he ordered Ali's passport revoked. The boxer was effectively barred from competing anywhere in the world.

As his appeal worked its way through the federal judicial system, eventually landing at the Supreme Court, Ali entered the speaking circuit in order to pay his bills. In 1968 he appeared at some two hundred college campuses, where he found some of his most receptive audiences. Though millions despised him for what they understood to be his "un-American" politics and religion, many young people gravitated toward his outspoken opposition to the war in Vietnam. "I'm not going to help nobody get something my Negroes don't have," Ali told one group of white college students during his speaking tour. "If I'm gonna die, I'll die now, right here, fighting you, if I'm gonna die. You my enemy. My enemy's the white people. Not Viet Cong, or Chinese, or Japanese. You my opposer when I want freedom. You my opposer when I want justice. You my opposer when I want equality. You won't even stand up for me in America for my religious beliefs, and you want me to go somewhere and fight, but you won't even stand up for me here at home."[45]

Since he first entered the American sports spotlight with his gold medal performance at the Rome Olympics, Ali's significance to American society had always exceeded his considerable place within the sport of boxing. At the age of twenty-six, he had already left a permanent mark on American sports culture. Even in exile, Muhammad Ali kept himself squarely in the public eye as the most visible antiwar advocate in the nation. In the spring of 1968, as Ali took his message to American cities and campuses across the country, heavyweight contenders positioned themselves for a shot at his vacated titles, and the presidential candidates, competing for an abdicated presidency, entered the height of campaign season.

two
Law and Order

Bobby Kennedy made several speeches on college campuses in the first weeks of his push for the Democratic nomination, addressing audiences that tended to be large, enthusiastic, and generally receptive to his antiwar message. Kennedy's first campaign stop after announcing his candidacy was a previously scheduled appearance at Kansas State University. There, he told a capacity crowd of mixed political persuasion that the nation was "deep in a malaise of spirit" and suffering from a "deep crisis of confidence." He also took an unusual step for a politician in acknowledging his own part, as a member of his brother's administration, in the escalating and increasingly unpopular war in Vietnam. "I am willing to bear my share of the responsibility, before history and before my fellow citizens," Kennedy told the crowd. "But past error is no excuse of its own perpetuation. Tragedy is a tool for the living to gain wisdom."[1]

After further criticism of Johnson's recalcitrant military strategy, Kennedy concluded, "Our country is in danger: not just from foreign enemies; but above all, from our own misguided policies—and what they can do to the nation that Thomas Jefferson once told us was the last, best hope of man. There is a contest on, not for the rule of America but for the heart of America. In these next eight months, we are going to decide what this country will stand for and what kind of men we are." He left the podium with a raised fist, and a thousand students soon enlisted to help with the upcoming Nebraska primary.[2]

Kennedy then went to Kansas University in Lawrence, where he spoke about poverty and domestic policy before a large crowd at Allen Fieldhouse. "Our Gross National Product, now, is over $800 billion a year," Kennedy said,

> but the Gross National Product—if we should judge America by that—counts air pollution and cigarette advertising, and ambulances to clear our highways of carnage. It counts special locks for our doors and the jails for those who break them. It counts the destruction of our redwoods and the loss of our natural wonder in chaotic sprawl. It counts napalm and the cost of a nuclear warhead . . . and the television programs which glorify violence in order to sell toys to our children. Yet the gross national product does not allow for the health of our children, the quality of their education, or the joy of their play. It does not include the beauty of our poetry or the strength of our marriages; the intelligence of our public debate or the integrity of our public officials. It measures neither our wit nor our courage . . . it measures everything, in short, except that which makes life worthwhile. And it can tell us everything about America except why we are proud that we are Americans."[3]

On the Republican side, Richard Nixon was a strong front-runner. Michigan governor George Romney (father of 2012 presidential candidate Mitt Romney) had once appeared to be Nixon's most formidable obstacle to the nomination. But Romney had dropped out before he could be annihilated in New Hampshire, where polls predicted that Nixon would beat him by sixty points. Voters and pundits found Romney pious and boring. The candidate was broadly derided for saying that he had been "brainwashed" into supporting the Vietnam War before rebranding himself as an antiwar Republican. Of course, the American government had in some sense deceived the entire nation about what was happening in southeast Asia. But Romney's choice of words did little to fill voters with confidence. *Time* magazine joked that perhaps Romney's brainwashing "could have been because he brought so light a load to the laundromat." Romney was a moderate in a polarized political moment, and his endorsement of President Johnson in the 1964 presidential race did not endear him to the Republican brass. Ohio governor James Rhodes put Romney's ineptitude rather bluntly when he said that "watching George Romney run for the presidency was like watching a duck try to make love to a football."[4]

After he received 11 percent of the New Hampshire vote on a write-in basis, liberal pockets of the Republican Party encouraged moderate New York governor Nelson Rockefeller to enter the race. He finally announced his candidacy on April 30, less than six weeks after declaring that he would not be running. Much had changed in those few weeks, including King's assassination and Johnson's decision not to run, and New York aristocrats and business leaders had convinced Rockefeller that Republicans needed an alternative to Nixon. He reasonably believed that he stood a better chance at winning the general election than Tricky Dick. A win in the Massachusetts primary on the day of his announcement gave Rockefeller supporters some initial hope. But Republican insiders were comfortable with Nixon, and Rockefeller's early indecision and his technocratic and patrician reputation prevented him from gaining enough national traction to derail the establishment candidate.

Out west, a quiet groundswell of support was building for political upstart Ronald Reagan, who had transformed himself, in less than two years, from an unlikely governor of California into a semiviable right-wing candidate for the Republican nomination. As biographer Bill Boyarsky explained, Reagan was "an evangelist warning of the destruction of the American dream [and] questioning the entire direction of American political life since the New Deal. . . . In a time of complexity, the voter looks for simple answers, and in Ronald Reagan he finds a spokesman and a leader."[5]

In crafting a public image for himself Reagan frequently referenced his bucolic childhood in small-town Illinois, where, he often recalled, "[he] learned the true riches of rags." After college, he was a sportscaster before heading to Hollywood to become an actor. His politics at that time, which tended toward New Deal liberalism, were a good fit for the Screen Actors Guild, of which he was president for six years. Reagan hosted *General Electric Theater*, a popular television anthology series, for eight years, and part of the job entailed traveling to GE plants to speak to employees. During his stint in the corporate behemoth's employ, he completed his political transformation, riding a wave of suburban fear of urban unrest to the California governorship in 1966. Wealthy backers pushed Reagan into the 1968 presidential campaign without any official declaration of candidacy, which would have violated his pledge not to use the governorship as a springboard to national office. He also avoided primaries because he didn't want to give the appearance of being divisive to the party. Republican leadership believed that a united front would prove an attractive contrast to the discombobulated Democrats.[6]

When heavy rain drove players from the course during practice rounds for the Masters at Augusta National Golf Club, some had watched coverage of the King funeral on the clubhouse television. Otherwise, the week's festivities at Augusta proceeded in typical fashion. There was no official acknowledgment of the slain leader laid to rest just a two-hour drive to the west. One member of the all-black caddie cadre at the club was asked if he planned to miss any time as a result of King's death. "I am very sympathetic to Dr. King," he replied. "But I'll be here. I got a family to feed."[7]

Financier Cliff Roberts and American golf hero Bobby Jones, Augusta National's founders, organized the Masters in 1934 to increase visibility for their new venture. The tournament had quickly risen from its modest Depression-era roots to rival the US Open as the most coveted prize in American golf. An inescapable element of Augusta National's identity was its capacity to call to mind aspects of the Old South. That association became an important, if understated, part of the club's signature event. The grand entrance to the grounds included a three-hundred-yard driveway lined with eighty-year-old magnolias leading to a large white antebellum-style mansion on land that had once been an indigo plantation. Every caddie, waiter, and locker room attendant was black and deferential. The club's members were all white men, and they included leading American industrialists and financiers who enjoyed traveling south during the winter and stepping back in time for golf and manly camaraderie.

In Augusta National's early days, fight nights held in the ballroom of the local Bon Air-Vanderbilt Hotel featured the "battle royale" exhibition in which blindfolded local black youths faced off in a boxing ring until only one was left standing. James Brown, whose family had moved to Augusta when he was a small child, and whose single "Say it Loud—I'm Black and I'm Proud" would hit the top ten in 1968, was a battle royale participant as a youngster. "I'd be out there stumbling around, swinging wild, and hearing people *laughing*," Brown later recalled. "I didn't know I was being exploited; all I knew I was getting paid a dollar and having fun."[8]

Sportswriter Grantland Rice helped Jones and Roberts publicize the club and its signature event in the early years. Accurately predicting that it would be easy to attract eastern and midwestern sportswriters returning from baseball's spring training in Florida, Rice recommended late March or early April for the tournament. Rice was born in 1889, the grandson of a Confederate officer, and he was arguably the most influential sports journalist of the first half of the twentieth century. His writing sounds decidedly overwrought to the modern ear. However, his words helped gild the heroes of the golden age of American sports in the 1920s—through Rice's promotion, athletes such as Babe Ruth, Bill Tilden, Bobby Jones, and Red Grange became familiar names. As a contemporary of Rice's put it, "If he couldn't say something nice about an athlete, he was likely to write about another athlete."[9]

Rice lent a modicum of dignity to sportswriting, a trade whose members' reputations had once been nearly as checkered as those of the athletes they covered. The fawning descriptions of athletes and athletics in Rice's era, which spanned five decades, helped broaden the appeal of sports in a society whose "respectable" citizens had once turned up their noses at that seedy world. American sports would look vastly different by the late 1960s. But Rice proved to be an asset for Jones and Roberts in getting their tournament some much-needed early exposure.

Charles de Clifford "Cliff" Roberts Jr. was born in southeastern Iowa in 1894 to an itinerate real estate speculator and his mentally unstable wife. The family moved often, and Roberts's early years were not particularly happy. Cliff's mother fatally shot herself when he was a teenager, and his father was later killed when he stepped in front of a train in what was officially deemed an accident. Roberts began his professional ascent as a suit salesman, then operated in oil and gas after his service in World War I. He subsequently parlayed a particularly lucrative sale of some mineral leases into a partnership stake in a Wall Street securities brokerage firm. As he began to ingratiate himself into New York society, Roberts nurtured a vision for a golf club in the South that could attract affluent easterners during the winter months. Augusta National was Roberts's idea. However, he needed Jones's fame and reputation to help draw the level of membership that would make the endeavor financially viable. The pair selected Augusta for its pleasant climate, good railroad access, and hotel options. Construction on Augusta National was completed in 124 days for $85,000. Jones named the club, but it was Roberts who named its signature event the Masters, an appellation Jones found pretentious.

The son of an Atlanta lawyer, Robert Tyre "Bobby" Jones Jr. took up golf after a series of childhood health problems had left him in poor physical condition. In a brilliant but brief career, Jones became one of the leading American athletes of the 1920s, winning four US Opens, three British Opens, five US Amateurs, and a British Amateur. He abruptly retired from competitive golf at the age of twenty-eight to focus on his Atlanta law practice and other interests that would soon include a world-class golf club in Augusta. Bobby Jones had been president of Augusta National since its founding, and he had once been called "the most popular southerner since Robert E. Lee and the most admired American athlete in the so-called Golden Age of Sport." Yet by 1968

Clifford Roberts, *chairman of the Masters Golf Tournament, and co-founder, with legendary American golfer Bobby Jones, of Augusta National Golf Club. (AP Photo)*

his health had been steadily deteriorating for two decades, and he wanted to die. Jones suffered from syringomyelia, a rare and painful neurological disorder affecting the spinal cord. This was the final Masters he would attend.[10]

Masters participants were required to use local caddies who were, by rule, black. Many of the Augusta National "loopers" were known by single colorful names, including Ironman, who always pulled the correct iron from the bag; Nubbins, whose fingers had been damaged by a meat grinder; Leven, the eleventh child in his family; and Stovepipe, who wore a distinctive hat.[11] By the late 1960s, writers started to notice that no black golfer had ever competed at Augusta. Charlie Sifford had won the 1967 Hartford Open, but he did not receive an invitation to the Masters the following year. It was unusual but not unprecedented for a tournament winner to not be invited—there had been twelve such instances since 1961. But Sifford also believed that his low early-round score that summer at the Canadian Open had prompted Masters officials to inform the Canadian tournament's host site that the Canadian winner would not automatically attend the next year's Masters. A notice to that effect was posted in the tournament locker room.

Frank Lett Sr., an African American columnist for the *Michigan Chronicle*, published an open letter to Cliff Roberts in February 1968 asking that Sifford be invited to play in the Masters. Lett also encouraged others to write the Augusta National chairman in support of Sifford, stating, "[Send letters] NOT because he is a Negro, but because he is a NEGRO GOLFER and has proven his ability to compete with the best. THERE NEVER HAS BEEN A NEGRO PLAYER in this prestigious event."[12]

Bobby Jones responded on Roberts's behalf and listed the standards the club applied in determining which golfers would receive invitations. He made reference to a couple of categories under which Sifford might still be invited. But Sifford was not invited, and critics were convinced that organizers were merely hiding behind their nominal criteria to justify their decisions. Frustrated regarding Sifford's plight, Jim Murray wrote in the *Los Angeles Times*, "The Masters golf tournament is as white as the Ku Klux Klan. Everybody on it can ride in the front of the bus." Black players' absence grew more conspicuous each year, eventually causing Cliff Roberts to respond, in 1972, "I don't know what you mean. We had that boy from Thailand last year and he was as black as the ace of spades."[13]

Murray was at the forefront of a new postwar generation of sportswriters whose work transcended mere description of games and hero worship of athletes. He wrote for *Time* magazine before joining *Sports Illustrated* in time for its inaugural issue in 1954. Murray also spent nearly forty years as a columnist for the *Los Angeles Times*, where he gained a national reputation for his snappy one-liners, including one about UCLA coach John Wooden being "so square [he was] divisible by four." Writing about politically sensitive issues was nearly unavoidable by the late sixties. Even so, Murray had been ahead of most of his contemporaries in treating sports as a window through which to observe broader aspects of society.[14]

As the players, fans, and press converged on Augusta for the start of the tournament, the leading contenders appeared to be Arnold Palmer and Jack Nicklaus. Palmer, the first star of golf's television era, had won four of the last ten Masters. Nicklaus, eleven years Palmer's junior and on the cusp of tour dominance, had captured three of the last five. But Palmer would miss the cut for the first time since 1955, and Nicklaus's third-round 74 dropped him out of serious contention. After three rounds, eight players were within two shots of the lead held by South African Gary Player. Affable Argentinian Roberto De Vicenzo was among the eight athletes on the tightest leaderboard in Masters history.[15]

De Vicenzo had won the previous year's British Open, becoming the oldest champion in the long history of the prestigious event. But at age forty-four he was on the tail end of a remarkable professional career that had begun when he was fifteen years old. In all, he would win more than two hundred professional tournaments on three continents, including forty-two national championships in more than a dozen countries. De Vicenzo's large nose and conspicuous bald spot made him recognizable even to casual fans. His warm and outgoing personality ingratiated him to many of the players on tour despite his imperfect command of the English language. He had an abbreviated swing, but his huge hands and forearms made him one of the longest hitters in the world. Despite having played at the Masters since 1950, De Vicenzo had trouble putting there and had never finished better than a tie for tenth. But as he approached the eighteenth tee box in Sunday's final round, he was tied with American Bob Goalby for the lead. A US Army veteran and former multisport star at Belleville Township High School in Illinois, Goalby was still on the course, two holes behind Roberto.

De Vicenzo's drive was straight but short on eighteen. The flag was in the front left of a three-tiered green that sloped severely toward the fairway. A large greenside bunker guarded the hole, making a shot aimed at the pin a dangerous one. His caddie, "Crosshanded" Henry Brown, suggested he swing a five iron toward the safety of the right side of the green. But Roberto chose a four iron, taking dead aim with a three-quarter swing.[16] He hooked it. The ball cleared the bunker and landed hole-high, left of the target. It took a leftward kick and came to rest in the gallery thirty feet from the hole. De Vicenzo then asked Brown for his putter and cagily knocked his ball to within six feet, leaving a tricky left-to-right breaker. He missed the par putt on the low side, settling for a bogey, which put him a shot behind Goalby.

Frustrated at the way he had finished his round, De Vicenzo sat down at the scorer's table, quickly recorded the scores of the final five holes for playing partner Tommy Aaron, and signed the scorecard. Then a green-jacketed official told Roberto that he was needed in the Butler Cabin for a television interview. "I sit down only one second and a guy in a green coat is behind me," De Vicenzo recalled. "The guy says, 'Come on Roberto, we gotta go to press room.' I think I go too quick." He glanced at the scores recorded for him by Aaron, signed that card, and was whisked to the television cameras to discuss his round.[17]

De Vicenzo had left the box for total score on the scorecard blank; players were responsible only for the score they recorded for each hole, not for adding up the totals. Before leaving the scorer's table, Aaron, a former All-America golfer and business major at the University of Florida, took a last look at De

Vicenzo's card and noticed an error. A tournament official had added the scores and written 66 for Roberto's total. Aaron knew that De Vicenzo had shot 65 and asked where Roberto had gone. Someone told him that he had jumped in a golf cart and was doing a TV interview. Aaron alerted an official to the problem.

Men with walkie-talkies scrambled into action. Soon Roberto reappeared, and chief rules official and former bank president Ike Grainger told him that his scorecard was incorrect. De Vicenzo had made a birdie three on the seventeenth hole, as thousands of witnesses and millions watching at home clearly saw. But Aaron had recorded a four for Roberto, and Roberto had attested to that score with his signature. Aaron pleaded for a chance to correct his clerical error. A squad of green jackets hurried to the cabin where the wheelchair-bound Bobby Jones was watching the television coverage. They explained the situation to him.

Grainger, an alumnus of Woodberry Forest School and Princeton, was once described by his nephew as a person "who went to sleep every night reading the rules of golf." Grainger read the applicable Rule 38-3 to Jones: "No alteration may be made on a card after the competitor has returned it to the Committee. If the competitor returns a score for any hole lower than he actually played, he shall be disqualified. A score higher than actually played must stand as returned." Jones saw no way to deviate from what appeared to be a very clear rule.[18]

Meanwhile, Goalby was finishing his round, unaware of the developing scorecard situation. Following a bogey on seventeen that dropped him back into a tie with Roberto, Goalby knocked a tricky downhill forty-five-foot putt that broke sharply left to right to within four feet on eighteen. The putt left him with a knee-knocking four-footer for par and what he and everyone watching believed would be a tie to force an eighteen-hole playoff the following day. For the first time all week, Goalby sought the advice of his caddie, Frank "Marble Eye" Stokes, who reported that he saw no break—nothing but the bottom of the cup. Goalby knocked it dead center and headed to the scorer's table.

As Goalby accepted congratulations on what he thought was a spot in a playoff, Ike Grainger returned from Bobby Jones's cabin to break the news to Roberto. There would be no leniency. A rule was a rule. Masters officials regretted the result that its enforcement yielded, but their hands were tied. Pat Summerall was anchoring his first Masters broadcast and had the unenviable task of explaining to the television audience why the jovial Argentinian, whom everyone had just seen finish in a tie for first place, had been officially declared the runner-up, one shot behind the champion Goalby.

Roberto De Vicenzo (left) *sits beside Masters winner Bob Goalby at Augusta National Golf Club after De Vicenzo's scorecard error cost the Argentinian a spot in a playoff. In the wake of the controversial conclusion to the tournament, American journalists debated the fairness and application of the rules of golf. Some writers saw the strange ending to the Masters as a reflection of broader trouble in American society. (AP Photo/File)*

Though there was no evidence of anything untoward, some of the caddies suspected a conspiracy to keep the foreigner from winning the Masters, particularly at the expense of a clean-cut American military vet. Mark Eubanks, who caddied for Canadian amateur Gary Cowen that year, remained convinced years later. "That was a setup! They didn't want no foreigner to win," he insisted. Carl Jackson, who had dropped out of school at thirteen, had begun caddying at Augusta at fourteen, and had won two Masters on Ben Crenshaw's bag, recalled, "My first thought was, 'They done tricked that man out of the Masters.' Being a minority in those days made you think they weren't too ready for a foreign winner."[19]

Tommy Aaron explained his mistake: "I realized I had made an error before I left the official table. I looked around for Roberto but he was gone. There was a general state of confusion. I wish I could have done something but the damage had been done—he had already signed."[20]

"I feel very sorry for me," Roberto told reporters. "I am so unhappy to make five on the last hole, and Bob, he gave me so much pressure on the last hole that I lose my brain. I play golf all over the world for thirty years, and now all I can think of is, what a stupid I am to be wrong in this wonderful tournament."[21]

Goalby was as gracious as perhaps he could have been under the circumstances. "I never thought I could win this tournament," he admitted to the press. "I've always played terrible here. The only thing I regret is the manner I won it, after the way Roberto played. I'm really deeply sorry we couldn't play it off tomorrow." Asked specifically about the rule, Goalby responded, "It's an unfortunate rule, but it's a correct rule." Players largely agreed with Goalby. Jack Nicklaus, who finished tied for fifth, said, "What can you do? The score is written down and the man signs it. I feel sorry for Roberto, but those are the rules. A rule is a rule." This reaction was almost certainly shared by millions of Americans who were tired of a society they believed was too often comfortable flouting laws. The widespread rioting and protests that had filled American public spaces in the past year exemplified this tendency. But others felt that the De Vicenzo decision was another example of injustice suffered at the hands of wealthy, powerful white men.[22]

"Don't offer us the lame 'rules are rules' excuse," sports editor of the *Cleveland Plain Dealer* Hal Lebovitz retorted. "Rules involve justice and common sense and your committee was guilty of ignoring both." Many commentators objected not to the rule but to the prelude to its enforcement. Gene Ward of the *New York Daily News* wrote, "At the scoring table behind the 18th green … were several high-ranking officials eminently versed in Rule No. 38, section 3. Not one of those officials around the scoring table of this great tournament bothered to check De Vicenzo's card. No one offered to help him in any way." Sandy Grady of the *Philadelphia Bulletin* doubted whether justice had been meted out impartially. "You wonder if all those green-coated officials enjoyed their bourbon last night, knowing De Vicenzo had been robbed in the nit-picking confusion. You also wonder if the same outrage would have been perpetrated upon those Augusta idols, Nicklaus or Palmer."[23]

Augusta National was flooded with telegrams criticizing the decision. "We've gotten quite a stack of them," chairman Roberts later acknowledged. "And not one said we did the proper thing. They all say, 'You gave that fellow a bum deal.' [But critics] don't understand the difference between golf and spectator sports, such as football and baseball. Baseball and football players have no responsibility about keeping score. In golf, this responsibility is pinned on the player." Roberts scoffed at the notion that a scorekeeper could be sent to accompany the players. "The playing partner is a much more qualified scorer than any young lady you could send around to keep score," he said.[24]

Some felt that De Vicenzo had not been wronged, and that Goalby was the real victim of the whole fiasco. Bill Beck of the *St. Louis Post-Dispatch* wrote, "Roberto, for all his charm, deprived Goalby of any chance for a clearcut championship [by failing to properly check his scorecard]. De Vicenzo could not have done so more effectively if he had birdied the eighteenth hole instead of bogeying it. If that had happened, Goalby still would have had recourse—his golf clubs and a matching birdie." Dick Hyland of the *Palm Desert Post* agreed. "De Vicenzo finished his final round while Bob Goalby was yet on the 18th tee and the Masters officials, from [Cliff] Roberts on down, KNEW Roberto had goofed, knew his round's legal score was 66 and not 65, knew Goalby needed but a par on 18 to win, a bogey to tie. They withheld that information from the official scoreboard. They denied Bob Goalby that important, vital information. That, to me, is awful. There can be no excuse."[25]

As the controversy spilled from the sports pages into popular culture, editorial departments tended to rally behind De Vicenzo. Beneath the headline "Tainted Tournament" the *Washington Post* opined, "To a country which has made rather a fetish of 'sportsmanship,' the outcome of last weekend's Masters golf tournament in Augusta, Ga., must bring a feeling of chagrin and shame. . . . Few sportsmen anywhere in the world will think that Roberto De Vicenzo was dealt with generously or even fairly." An editorial in the *New York Times* asked, "Where in golf is justice; and are the gods of the green without mercy?"[26]

Americans who sympathized with Roberto needed someone to blame for his mistreatment. Cliff Roberts was not sufficiently visible, Jones was a dying icon, and the rules committee was too impersonal. Many fans thus assigned guilt to Goalby. He received over five hundred pieces of hate mail in the wake of his Masters win. One writer declared, "[I should] put you and that bastard Sonny Liston in concrete and drop you both in the Atlantic Ocean." Another said he hoped Goalby would "burn in hell for all eternity."[27]

Goalby felt that the controversy had denied him the credit he deserved for his Masters victory. "I've always felt like a victim, as much or more than Roberto," he would say two decades later. "None of the problems with the scorecards were my fault. But I have forever been singled out as the guy who won the Masters because of some damn clerical mistake. I don't think I ever got credit for what I did that week."[28] On the presidential campaign trail, Richard Nixon capitalized on an analogous sentiment. Millions of voters felt that the nation focused too heavily on the nominally disadvantaged rather than on the people who followed the rules and who had ridden the wave of postwar economic prosperity that seemed to be subsiding.

Sports journalists' and editorialists' reactions to the unusual conclusion to the Masters fueled Americans' perception that their society was becoming ever more polarized. As golf historian Curt Sampson observes, "Americans in the late 60s labeled each other and themselves constantly, a bumper-sticker mentality that assumed an opinion on one topic indicated an entire world-view. We called each other hard hat or hippie, peacenick or redneck, freak or crew cut. The dinner-table defender of Goalby had to be pro-Vietnam War, anti-protest, My Country Right or Wrong. If you thought De Vicenzo had gotten a raw deal, you must also be a draft card-, flag-, or brassiere burner. It was an angry atmosphere that allowed people to be incredibly or stupidly wrong about almost everything, in print or at the top of their lungs." [29]

Certainly not everyone who defended Goalby favored Nixon's law-and-order rhetoric or military escalation in Vietnam. In a less tense cultural moment, news of the Masters' outcome might not have drawn such inflammatory opinions. But those strong reactions from columnists and pundits illustrated a growing mutual suspicion on the opposing sides of an increasingly politicized and polarized American society. In that context, Vice President Hubert Humphrey's speech announcing his entry into the presidential race later that month struck many as tone-deaf. "Here we are," Humphrey told 1,700 supporters at the Shoreham Hotel in Washington, DC, "the way politics ought to be in America, the politics of happiness, the politics of purpose, the politics of joy. And that's the way it's going to be all the way, from here on in." [30]

Politics of joy were not visible at Columbia University, where confrontational student demonstrations culminated in the occupation of five buildings on the New York City campus days before Humphrey declared his candidacy. The protesters objected to the university's plan to build a gymnasium in city-owned Morningside Park, as well as the school's involvement with the Institute for Defense Analyses (IDA), a war industries think tank affiliated with the Department of Defense. The park in which the proposed gym was to be built was bordered on one side by the Ivy League university's campus and on the other side by Harlem, whose residents would have only limited access to the gym though it would occupy public property. The project thus earned the nickname "gym crow."

The occupation began when baton-wielding police chased an assemblage of demonstrators from the gym construction site. The mob made its way to Hamilton Hall, the ivy-covered main building of Columbia's undergraduate college, where students demanded to see "The Man."[31] The protests and occupations lasted a week, and they eventually spread to other buildings and splintered along racial lines. In the early morning of April 30, a thousand police stormed five occupied buildings on the order of Republican mayor John Lindsay, who harbored hopes of a possible vice presidential nomination. Seven hundred students were arrested and at least a hundred were injured in what the student newspaper called "a brutal bloody show of strength."[32]

On the presidential campaign trail, Republicans and Democrats criticized the Columbia students. Richard Nixon called the protests "a national tragedy and a national disgrace," while Vice President Humphrey told supporters at a Pennsylvania campaign rally, "[Campus disruptions] make me sick all the way through."[33] For many Americans, student protests were yet another sign— along with urban riots, soft-on-crime judges, sexual promiscuity, antiwar demonstrations, government programs inordinately benefiting minorities, long-haired hippies, and drug use—that society had come off its rails. But Columbia protesters ultimately achieved their two main objectives; the school abandoned its gym construction plans and severed ties with the IDA. And the protests inspired and emboldened hundreds of thousands of students who would demonstrate in favor of and against various causes on North American and western European campuses that year.

City leaders in Louisville watched the national news with trepidation as the first Saturday in May approached. First run in 1875, the Kentucky Derby featured a long history, national visibility, cultural significance, and evocation of the antebellum South that made it an attractive target for protesters. Officials at Churchill Downs hoped their racetrack would not become a site of conflict as it had the year before. In 1967 national civil rights leaders had gathered in Louisville during Derby Week to protest the city's historically discriminatory housing policies and to advocate for a fair-housing ordinance.

In a gesture of solidarity with the protesters, five teenagers ran onto the racetrack at Churchill Downs the week of the 1967 Derby, narrowly avoiding ten horses rumbling down the homestretch. The young men survived the stunt uninjured, diving into the infield as the Thoroughbreds galloped by. But threats of disruption caused the cancellation of the city's Pegasus Parade, a popular Derby Week fixture. Open-housing advocates threatened more action if their demands were not met. "No open housing, no Derby" became a rallying cry for the protesters, but Mayor Kenneth Schmied assured the city that the Derby would not be disturbed. "The Kentucky Derby is one of the world's greatest sporting events," the mayor declared, "and we will do everything possible to see that it is run in its richest tradition."[34]

Kentucky governor Edward T. Breathitt had been even more forceful in his assurances, promising to do "whatever [was] necessary" to make certain that the event would not be disturbed. "The Derby must be run," Breathitt told the director of the state police. "It is our state's showcase. We're on national television. We're going to have 100,000 people coming through the gates at Churchill. The race is a huge economic entity. Tell me what you need, and we'll get it for you."[35]

National organizations as varied as the Southern Christian Leadership Conference and the Ku Klux Klan flocked to the spotlight of Derby Week in Louisville in 1967. Klan leaders offered to keep order at the racetrack and promised to bring thousands of their brethren to Louisville to help. "The Kentucky Derby is an important national event," a Klansman explained, "and we don't see that it has anything to do with open housing. We suggest that they either bar Negroes from Churchill Downs Saturday or find some other way to control them."[36]

Late that Friday, protest organizers including Martin Luther King Jr. and his brother Rev. A. D. Williams King, pastor at Louisville's Zion Baptist Church, announced that they would hold a rally away from Churchill Downs and that there would be no disruption at the Derby itself. Louisville's leading African American newspaper, the *Louisville Defender*, supported the decision, praising King's "good judgment." Despite those assurances, track officials were ready with plenty of law enforcement, including 2,500 National Guard soldiers. Troops encircled the racetrack as post time neared and received orders to hit any fence jumpers in the head. "Only a few Negroes were in the big infield," the *Louisville Courier-Journal* noted, "and they appeared to go unnoticed by the crowd. What tension there was appeared directed at badges and helmets." On the track, a 30–1 long shot named Proud Clarion defeated heavily favored Damascus in one of the biggest upsets of the era.[37]

The Pegasus Parade returned to Louisville in 1968. A "happy but well-behaved" crowd of two hundred thousand lined the streets and saw Louisville native Jimmy Ellis serve as grand marshal. Ellis had recently earned national acclaim by winning a tournament determining who would assume the WBA boxing championship stripped from Muhammad Ali, his former sparring partner. "We want to show Jimmy how much his home town appreciates his hard work in bringing the heavyweight title back to Kentucky," said Basil Caummisar, president of the Kentucky Derby Festival Committee.[38]

Two colts had emerged as favorites for the 1968 Derby: Dancer's Image, a handsome gray owned by a Massachusetts car dealer whose father had once been governor of the Bay State; and Calumet Farm's powerful bay Forward Pass. No stable had won more Kentucky Derbies than Calumet. But that venerable outfit—which baking-powder magnate William Wright had founded in 1924, and which his son Warren transformed into a Thoroughbred-racing juggernaut in the 1940s and '50s—had not had a Derby starter in a decade. For Fuller, having a horse in the Derby was a new experience altogether.

Fuller's father, Alvan Tufts Fuller, had left school at sixteen, then worked in a rubber factory and dabbled in bicycle racing and repair before selling his racing trophies to finance a trip to Europe. There, the elder Fuller had bought two automobiles that would form the foundation for his dealership in Boston that would become one of the most successful in the world. He was an early innovator of the idea of "buying on time" and of trading old cars for credit toward new ones. Alvan Fuller also used his business success as a springboard into politics, serving in the Massachusetts state legislature and the US House of Representatives before becoming governor of Massachusetts in 1925. After two terms as governor, Fuller returned to his automobiles and art collecting.[39]

Upon graduating from Harvard, Peter Fuller pursued a boxing career before joining his father in the car business. He became involved in horse racing in the early 1950s, and in 1964 he made his first visit to the Kentucky Derby, where he watched Northern Dancer win in record time. He was impressed by the performance and decided to breed his mare Noor's Image to the Derby winner's maternal grandfather, Native Dancer, the most expensive stallion in the world, who stood at A. G. Vanderbilt Jr.'s Sagamore Farm outside Baltimore. The resulting foal was Dancer's Image.

During his successful two-year-old season, Dancer's Image was named champion in Canada. The colt had uneven results as a three-year-old before trainer Lou Cavalaris decided to remove his blinkers and enlist the services of 1967 Kentucky Derby–winning jockey Bobby Ussery. With the Triple Crown as its ultimate goal, the Dancer's Image team hoped that a broader field of vision without the blinkers would help the colt to run from off the pace in the spring's longer races. Dancer's Image validated his trainer's foresight with a strong win in the $100,000 Governor's Cup at Bowie Racetrack in Maryland two days after Martin Luther King's death. Ussery let the colt settle at the back of the pack before unleashing a powerful rally in the homestretch to win by three lengths. The horse's time was only one-fifth of a second off the track record. Fuller had met the slain civil rights leader and his recently widowed wife on at least one occasion, and he told his farm manager before the race that he planned to donate any winnings to Coretta Scott King.

Two weeks later, Dancer's Image again charged from the back of the field to win the Wood Memorial at Aqueduct in Queens, again in near-record time, in his final Derby prep. During CBS's coverage of the race, television announcer Win Elliot mentioned Fuller's donation to King's widow. The gesture would seem to have been innocuous and generous on the surface. But that gift (more than $60,000 for the winner's share) elicited criticism from many sports fans, particularly in Kentucky, where some recalled King's involvement in protests that had threatened to disturb the Derby the previous year. A writer for the *Thoroughbred Record*, for example, declared that by giving money to Mrs. King, Fuller had "made a mistake of injecting the racial situation into thoroughbred racing."[40]

Fuller believed that the gift turned many in Louisville against him. "It became something that it should not have become," Fuller said, noting that the negative response caught him by surprise. "[The gift] was just my way of saying, 'Hell, this was a hell of a guy,' and I'd say that to any redneck in the world," he explained. "It's something I just felt very strongly about. It was an opportunity for a white man to show that he could sympathize with the Negro."[41]

With his win in the Wood, Dancer's Image cemented his place among the top Derby contenders. The only horse receiving more attention as the big race neared was Calumet Farm's Forward Pass, winner of the Florida Derby and Blue Grass Stakes. Horses owned by Calumet had won seven Kentucky Derbies in the 1940s and '50s, an era when both the Derby and the famous farm were celebrated as exemplars of American strength, success, and durability. In the course of the Derby's long history, sports journalists had periodically gravitated toward its romantic aspects, particularly during times of domestic discord. The mint juleps, ladies in anachronistic hats, and antebellum anthem "My Old Kentucky Home" evoked what many white folks imagined to be a simpler and happier time in American history. Mixing romanticism with starker references grounded in bleaker realism, Jim Murray added another entry to that canon in his 1968 Derby column for the *Los Angeles Times*:

It's the most uniquely American event of all. It is redolent of Stephen Foster, who died in a waterfront flophouse, and who left America his bittersweet airs of magnolia and losers, and the sounds of banjos in the sick-sweet night downwind of the cotton.

So they run this one race a year, and all of a sudden it's the turn of the century again and sternwheelers are paddling down the long muddy rivers and the bales are piled up on the levees, and the hogsheads nod in the afternoon sun 'til the whiskey in them bubbles.

It's an evocative race. It belongs back in the time when trains whistled mournfully through the long hot nights, when ladies wore crinoline and a guy brought a horse to a race on a long rope and not in a six-wheel van.

It's just the seventh race on the program at this old weather-blown pile of overpainted rotten lumber—a dowager among racetracks, an old riverboat bawd that doesn't belong in this century at all.[42]

In the days leading up to the Derby, Peter Fuller worked to secure some sixty tickets for the large entourage he planned to bring with him to Kentucky. When Churchill Downs officials scoffed at what they felt was an outlandish request, Fuller sought help from horseman Warner L. Jones Jr., chairman of the race-track's board of directors. After Jones assured him he would do what he could to accommodate the Massachusetts contingent, Fuller asked about security for Dancer's Image. In the wake of his gift to Mrs. King, Fuller had received threatening letters, and he feared for his colt's safety. Jones disabused him of his idea to bring some Boston strong men to guard the barn and assured him that Churchill Downs had top-notch security. He also recommended that Fuller contact veterinarian Alex Harthill to look after his horse during Derby Week.

Harthill and Jones were old friends. "We'd go out to Warner's place on Sunday afternoons, way before there was Sunday racing," Harthill recalled. "We'd drink whiskey and have bare-knuckle fistfights, just for the fun of it." Harthill seemed to know everyone around the racetrack, and he hosted a broad swath of equestrian society at his Louisville home during Derby Week.[43]

Harthill met Dancer's Image at the airport ten days before the Derby. The colt was vanned to Churchill Downs and put in stall 7 in Barn 24, where beaten favorite Damascus had been housed the previous year. Everyone around the backstretch called it the Harthill Barn because Dr. Harthill, a brilliant fourth-generation veterinarian, kept his office there. A Churchill official rationalized the unusual arrangement as "sorta like squatter's rights." After graduating from Ohio State in 1948, Harthill had taken Ben Jones, trainer and later general manager for Calumet Farm, as one of his first clients. In his first year on the job Harthill treated Triple Crown winner Citation and saved the life of future Derby winner Ponder, who had suffered a serious chest injury when a groom carrying a pitchfork startled him. In his two decades of veterinary practice, Harthill also claimed to have treated a nearly unfathomable collection of Derby winners—Hill Gail, Dark Star, Swaps, Iron Liege, Tim Tam, Carry Back, Decidedly, Northern Dancer, Lucky Debonair, and, most recently, long shot Proud Clarion. The trail of rumors and innuendo related to Harthill's purported penchant for stretching the rules of racing was nearly as long.[44]

Dancer's Image's trainer Lou Cavalaris arrived in Louisville two days after his colt, one week before the Derby. When he got to the barn, Cavalaris learned that the colt had tweaked his chronically troublesome right front ankle. X-rays were negative, but Dr. Harthill recommended a dose of "Bute" to reduce inflammation. Around 10:30 on Sunday, Dancer's Image received a standard dose of Butazolidin, a trade name for the nonsteroidal anti-inflammatory analgesic phenylbutazone, similar to aspirin. "That was the only time that week he got anything from me," Harthill later said. "But hell, Lou and I went way back. If Lou had asked me to give the horse strychnine, I would have."[45]

Developed in 1946 for humans, Bute was commonly used in horses by the early '50s, and racing authorities began testing for it by the end of the decade. In 1962 Kentucky became the last major racing jurisdiction to ban it for use on race day. Yet no horse in the state had been disqualified for a positive test since Bute had become regulated. The drug could be administered during training, but not a trace could be in a horse's system during competition. The seventy-two-hour withdrawal time should have given the Sunday dose plenty of time to clear Dancer's Image's system before the Derby, though he would no longer be considered for Tuesday's Derby Trial Stakes.[46]

As Derby day approached, Fuller shared his confidence with anyone who would listen. "We're going to win the Derby," he told a reporter for the *Courier-Journal.* "I've told that to people, and they say, 'My God, here's another new one with a lot of money and not much sense.' But this is it. This is the quintessence. The Derby is what it's all about. I could be like some first-timers and say it'd sure be nice to finish fourth. But I'm in business. I'm going to tell it the way it is, pal, and the way it is is this: I know the Derby is made for this horse. I'm here to win."[47]

After a final pre-Derby workout on Friday, Harthill gave Dancer's Image a small dose of Azium, a (legal) steroid with anti-inflammatory effects. "He looks fine, but we'll know more tonight," Cavalaris told the press. "In the past, at times, his right front ankle has swollen to some extent and then gone down. He'll stand in ice, will be done up in liniment for the night. We'll gallop him tomorrow morning and if he isn't right we won't run him. He's too nice a horse for that. But I think he's gonna be all right. I'm optimistic." [48]

Mixing political business with pleasure, Richard Nixon traveled to Kentucky for the Derby and the attendant festivities. He was keen to build on Republican Barry Goldwater's southern success in the 1964 presidential election. Nixon spent the morning with Kentucky governor Louie B. Nunn, the first Republican elected to that office since World War II. Their social rounds included breakfast at Spindletop Hall, a luxurious Georgian revival–style mansion outside Lexington. "I wanted to see how rural America lived," Nixon said to Nunn upon arrival. "You call this a poverty area?" When the party arrived at Churchill Downs, Nixon had a few canned lines for the press. "We're here for another kind of race today," he said. "Both Democrats and Republicans can win this one." The candidate did more handshaking than handicapping and was more excited about the famous prerace song than about the horses. "I wanted to be here when the band played 'My Old Kentucky Home,'" he told reporters. "I watch the Derby on television about every year and I think that's the best part of the whole program."[49]

Dancer's Image had x-rayed clean after a nice gallop that morning, and Dr. Harthill had declared the colt ready to go. One hundred thousand voices sang "My Old Kentucky Home" as fourteen horses paraded in front of the grandstand on their way to the starting line. When the gates opened, Kentucky Sherry broke quickly from stall 4 and darted to the front. From the far outside, long shot Gleaming Sword swerved to the inside, knocking into Forward Pass, momentarily jarring the post-time favorite off his stride. But the big bay colt recovered quickly and joined the leaders as the herd passed the grandstand for the first time. Wearing Calumet's famous devil's red and blue silks, Milo Valenzuela rode Forward Pass aggressively as he chased Kentucky Sherry. The latter horse set a suicidal pace on the lead, nearly matching the track record for six furlongs.

Through the backstretch, Forward Pass sat within striking distance of the lead. Dancer's Image remained outside the frame of millions of television sets tuned to the broadcast, unhurried as he began his progress toward the front of the pack. "I was trying to get position going down the backside," Ussery said after the race. "I went inside a couple of horses, then outside a couple to get in the clear for a little way. But this horse seems to run better when he's behind horses, and I moved him back to the rail."[50]

Ussery urged Dancer's Image past tiring rivals on the final turn, and Forward Pass overtook pacesetter Kentucky Sherry as the field entered the homestretch. But the Calumet colt dawdled upon making the lead, and Dancer's Image popped through a gap on the inside and coasted past him to win by a length and a half. Ussery crossed the finish line, in the words of a reporter, "with a hippie haircut and a hippie grin, waving two fingers at the crowd." Perhaps misinterpreted as a peace sign, the jockey's manual gesture was a reference to his second consecutive Derby win. Only two other riders, African Americans Jimmy Winkfield and Isaac Murphy, had accomplished this feat. Both of them rode in the late nineteenth and early twentieth centuries, when black jockeys dominated the highest levels of the sport before being unofficially banned in the early 1900s.[51]

Jockey Bobby Ussery on Dancer's Image*, with owner Peter Fuller (left) and trainer Lou Cavalaris. Fuller believed that a hostile response to his gift to Coretta Scott King may have played a role in his horse's positive drug test. (AP Photos)*

In the winner's circle, Fuller was elated. "It's just great!" he shouted. "You couldn't dream it! Just look at all these wonderful people waving and applauding. It's just wonderful. The most wonderful week of my life." As the official photographs were concluding, Richard Nixon sidled up to Fuller. "Well, I guess we're one big Republican family here," Nixon said, gesturing to Fuller and Governor Nunn.

"Actually, my father was sort of an independent Republican," Fuller replied.

"Well, there's nothing partisan about horse racing anyway, I say," Nixon said with a photographer-ready grin still stuck on his face.[52]

Assistant trainer Robert Barnard accompanied Dancer's Image to the "spit box," where, per Kentucky rules of racing, a postrace urine sample was collected and taken to a private lab with a state contract. Early Monday morning, Kentucky's head racing chemist, Kenneth Smith, reported a positive result, indicating the presence of Bute, to Churchill Downs racing stewards. Track president Wathen Knebelkamp told the press, "We consider this a tragic misfortune. It shows, however, that people in racing are on their toes at all times and that it is a well-policed sport."[53]

Fuller was infuriated but not sure whom he should blame or what he could do. "Winning the Kentucky Derby was the most fantastic thrill I've ever had," he told reporters. "And this experience today is by far the biggest disappointment." Later, he expressed doubts about the security on Churchill Downs's backside, implying that something nefarious had perhaps caused the positive test. "I don't want to poke holes in racing, but this sort of security is enough to make a cat laugh." Fuller had continued to receive threatening mail related to his donation to Coretta King, including a telegram following the Derby that read, "SUGGEST YOU GIVE THE DERBY PURSE TO EITHER RAP BROWN OR STOKELY CARMICHAEL."[54]

Though they had no specific evidence, the Fuller camp became convinced that someone had "gotten to" Dancer's Image. "I think [the gift to Mrs. King] offended a lot of people," Fuller's daughter told the Associated Press as the fortieth anniversary of the incident approached in 2008. "That's basically why the horse got disqualified. The horse was a Maryland-bred. My dad was a Northerner. I think definitely that all factored in. . . . Hopefully someone will come out with the whole story, but I don't know if there's anyone that knows the whole story." Dr. Harthill was a person of suspicion for those seeking a suspect. The veterinarian gave Churchill Downs director of security Alvin Schem an official statement acknowledging that he had administered Bute, but he insisted that the dose should have long cleared the horse's system by Derby day.[55]

Public reaction to the scandal was mixed, but many racing journalists came down squarely in the "law-and-order" camp, viewing the situation through politicized lenses. "So long as a rule is in the books, it ought to be respected—even if it's a rule against mare's milk," wrote *Thoroughbred Record* editor William Robertson. "The rule should not be changed merely because it pinches at the moment. A rule which *never* pinches is worthless. . . . There is ample opinion that the ban against [Bute] is no good. I happen to feel that it is not as bad as the free use of the drug would be. On the other hand, it seems to be the fashion nowadays to literally wallow in self-criticism. When rioters riot and looters loot, it is not the fault of the rioters and looters but the fault of the 'system' controlled by non-rioters and non-looters, who thereupon are expected to engage in morbid introspection and go into fits of penitence. Nuts to that."

Sports Illustrated called the incident "the story of the year," and Walter Cronkite was prepared to air a report beneath the headline "Derby Winner a Hop-Head" until a racing correspondent explained that the drug did not actually "hop" a horse.[56]

The Monday after the test results were released, a three-day stewards hearing began. After eleven witnesses and twelve hundred pages of testimony, the stewards determined that Dancer's Image had won the Kentucky Derby with phenylbutazone in his system. The purse was to be redistributed. Fuller appealed the ruling to the Kentucky State Racing Commission, but he had little reason for optimism. That body had never overturned a stewards' ruling.[57]

The commission was a five-person board appointed by Governor Nunn, who had lamented the "crumbling of law and order" and "the traditional American way of life" in an address to the Kentucky Broadcasters Association earlier that year. The chairman of the commission was Louisville businessman George Egger, who had served as finance chair of Nunn's gubernatorial campaign. The other members were respected owners and breeders with a collective reputation for integrity.[58]

The Kentucky Racing Commission ultimately affirmed the stewards' decision. The long appellate process that ensued would cost Fuller a quarter-million dollars in legal fees, and it did nothing to alter the commission's ruling or Fuller's belief that he had been cheated. "I mean, baby doll, the Civil War was still pretty good down there," Fuller later said. "I was the new guy in the game from abolitionist Boston. I've heard from people there who say we absolutely got screwed and from other people who say, 'please, Peter, shut up and go away.'"[59]

Lurleen Wallace, wife of the third-party presidential candidate, succumbed to cancer three days after Dancer's Image crossed the wire first in the Kentucky Derby. She had been elected governor of Alabama less than two years earlier, succeeding her husband, who retained effective power while circumventing a state prohibition of consecutive gubernatorial terms. The couple's marriage was not a particularly happy one. After a mourning period of five weeks, Lurleen's passing freed George Wallace to wage a more vigorous national campaign.[60]

Wallace knew he had little realistic chance at the presidency, but he harbored reasonable hopes that he could garner enough support to throw the electoral decision to Congress. News from pollster George Gallup the day of Mrs. Wallace's death bolstered those hopes. Gallup reported, "If the presidential election were being held today, the strong possibility exists that third-party candidate George Wallace would deny either major party candidate the electoral votes needed to win." With reports of protests and violence filling newspapers through the spring and summer, Wallace's talk of "law and order" fueled his slow, steady rise in national polls.[61]

three
Where Have You Gone . . . ?

Many of Bobby Kennedy's closest advisors had told him not to run for president. Jackie Kennedy feared "the same thing that happened to Jack" would happen to Bobby. "There is so much hatred in this country," she explained, "and more people hate Bobby than hated Jack." But Bobby Kennedy determined that he "had no choice" but to run once Lyndon Johnson indicated he would continue to wage war in Vietnam. Critics scoffed at Kennedy's claims of moral obligation, certain that he had entered the race because he believed he could win, rather than for any nobler objective. But Kennedy was delivering a new kind of message that resonated with idealistic youths. And though he faced opposition from party bosses, union leaders, the business community, white southerners, and the conservative and liberal wings of the Democratic Party, he slowly built momentum and drew passionate crowds to his speeches.

Many of the journalists who covered Kennedy's early campaign stops also fell under his spell, though most seriously doubted he could win the nomination. Some even wondered whether he would live until November. *New York*

Post columnist Jimmy Breslin was among a pool of reporters gathered at a restaurant following another rousing Kennedy speech. "Do you think this guy has the stuff to go all the way?" Breslin asked his table.

"Yes, of course he has the stuff to go all the way," *Newsweek*'s John Lindsey replied. "But he's not going to go all the way. The reason is that someone is going to shoot him. I know it and you know it. Just as sure as we're sitting here somebody is going to shoot him."[1]

Kennedy was well aware of the mortal risk he assumed by campaigning for president. "There is no way to protect a candidate during the campaign," he said. "I know that there will be an attempt on my life sooner or later. Not so much for political reasons, but through contagion, through emulation." Yet he took a fatalistic approach to that risk. "There's just no reason worrying about those things," he told an Associated Press reporter. "If they want to, they can get you." He explained that his only real worry would be his children's welfare. After a long pause, he added, "This really isn't such a happy existence, is it?"[2]

Kennedy followed a win in the Indiana primary in early May with a landslide victory in Nebraska the following week. Those strong performances demonstrated that the Kennedy political brand still had national appeal, but early positive momentum was not enough to convince McCarthy to leave the race, or to dislodge Vice President Hubert Humphrey from his status as the most likely Democratic nominee. In mid-May, the campaigns moved west for primaries in Oregon, California, and South Dakota. Kennedy struggled in Oregon, where there was little poverty or racial strife. "I appeal best to people who have problems," he noted. "Everyone is too comfortable here." He also stood firm in his support for gun control legislation, even in the gun-loving Beaver State. In a speech touting a specific gun control measure, he told a crowd, "All the legislation does is keep guns from criminals, and the demented and those too young. With all the violence and murder and killings we've had in the United States, I think you will agree that we must keep firearms from people who have no business with guns or rifles." Many did not agree. Kennedy lost the Oregon primary by six points, becoming the first in his family to lose an election.[3]

But he rebounded with wins in California and South Dakota a week later, on June 4, to conclude his primary push on a seemingly strong note. In California, solid black and Hispanic turnout overcame McCarthy's strong suburban backing. The election results reinvigorated Kennedy as he waited in his fifth-floor suite at the Ambassador Hotel in Los Angeles. He told friends, "I feel now for the first time that I've shaken off the shadow of my brother. I feel I made it on my own."[4]

Kennedy addressed reporters and supporters near midnight in the hotel's packed Embassy Ballroom. He spoke for fifteen minutes, first acknowledging Dodgers pitcher Don Drysdale's sixth-straight shutout, then thanking everyone from his staff to his family to his dog Freckles. He repeated a campaign theme regarding "certain obligations and responsibilities to our fellow citizens" and concluded by saying, "So my thanks to all of you, and now it's on to Chicago and let's win there." He gave the crowd a thumbs-up, then a two-fingered victory sign, before self-consciously fixing his hair and leaving the stage.[5]

A hotel employee ushered Kennedy through a kitchen corridor on his way to a press conference in another room. The candidate shook hands with kitchen staff and answered questions from a radio reporter before Sirhan Bishara Sirhan emerged from the crowd and yelled, "Kennedy, you son of a bitch" as he fired a .22-caliber pistol at Kennedy's head. Born in Jerusalem to Arab Christian parents, Sirhan had immigrated to the United States when he was twelve, settling in Southern California with his family. After dropping out of Pasadena City College he had hoped to become a jockey. He worked as a hotwalker at Santa Anita racetrack, cooling out horses after their morning gallops, before landing a job as an exercise rider at a nearby ranch. But head and eye injuries suffered in a fall caused him to reevaluate his professional ambitions. Sirhan later claimed that Kennedy's support for Israel had motivated him to kill the senator. Yet Kennedy was hardly outside the American mainstream in his positions on Middle East politics. Witnesses at the Ambassador Hotel later told the FBI that they had heard Sirhan complaining about "rich people" and condemning Kennedy's attempt to "buy the presidency."[6]

As Kennedy lay dying, journalist Jack Newfield told civil rights leader John Lewis, "I can feel history slipping through my fingers." Lewis had been a close associate of Martin Luther King but had not wept at that leader's killing. At Kennedy's death, however, he sobbed "as if something had been busted open inside." A columnist for the *Philadelphia Enquirer* lamented, "This country does not work anymore. Maybe it stopped the day John Kennedy was killed, and only we did not know it at the time."[7]

After a requiem Mass at St. Patrick's Cathedral in New York, a twenty-one-car funeral train carried Kennedy's body to Washington, DC, on June 8 for his burial at Arlington National Cemetery. Along the 226-mile path a million people lined the tracks. More than a thousand passengers filled the train, including Coretta Scott King, Jackie Kennedy, and various friends, relatives, celebrities, and dignitaries. Penn Central closed all other traffic on the line after a northbound express struck at least six people paying their respects in

Sen. Robert F. Kennedy *addressing supporters at the Ambassador Hotel in Los Angeles early in the morning of June 5, 1968, following his victory in the California presidential primary election. Moments later, he would be fatally shot in a kitchen corridor as he spoke to a radio reporter, dying the next day. (AP Photo/Dick Strobel)*

Elizabeth, New Jersey. Two were killed, and four were seriously wounded. Thereafter the funeral train proceeded at half speed, allowing passengers to get a good look at the multitudes of mourners.

Republicans and Democrats clashed over the meaning and significance of Kennedy's death. Republicans discerned a need for more law and order in America. California governor Ronald Reagan falsely told an audience, "In this week of tragedy, six policemen in Chicago [were] killed in the line of duty." In fact, only two had been killed on the job the entire calendar year. Democrats saw the assassination as evidence that America was drowning in violence and alienation. President Johnson addressed the nation from the White House when it became apparent that Kennedy would not survive. After the deaths of John Kennedy and Martin Luther King, Johnson had pressed Congress to approve legislation concerning civil rights and fair housing. The president used Robert Kennedy's high-profile killing to again call for governmental action: "Let the Congress pass laws to bring the insane traffic in guns to a halt, as I have appealed to them time and time again to do. This will not, in itself, end the violence, but reason and experience tell us that it will slow it down; that it will spare many innocent lives."[8]

The politicization of the murder predictably spilled into the realm of sports. Hours after Kennedy's death, Howard Cosell eulogized the slain leader on his radio show, eliciting a stream of calls from angry listeners. "Don't tell me how to live," one caller said. "Just give us the scores, that's what you're paid for." Vin Scully, radio announcer for the Los Angeles Dodgers, opened his broadcast the night of Kennedy's death by saying, "They say the eye of the storm is the quiet part, and here, Dodger Stadium, has suddenly become the eye of the storm—a large crowd, approximately 50,000, and the winds of all kinds of emotions swirling around the ballpark. Certainly there are still the winds of sorrow; what a dreadful, drab and heartbreaking day it has been. But as the gray skies now slowly start to disappear to night, so, too, the feelings in the ballpark are turning. And from almost the pits of despair, we concentrate on a child's game—a ball, a bat and some people hitting it, throwing it and catching it."[9]

As Robert Lipsyte noted in the *New York Times* the day of the funeral, "In amassing perhaps the largest group of committed athletes to support a contender for candidacy, the Kennedy camp was criticized for appealing to younger voters and black voters in an emotional and unreasonable way. Although athletes have supported and actively campaigned for every one of the other major candidates, only Kennedy went out of his way to include them in as a group, and only Kennedy provided an instant expression for the growing political involvement of athletes. [They believed] that Senator Kennedy was a candidate who could translate their own energy and need for acclaim, their emerging sense of social responsibility and growing militancy into a team victory." Some of the most famous athletes in America had supported Kennedy, including Oscar Robertson, Bill Russell, Hank Aaron, Gayle Sayers, and Stan Musial.[10]

The best pitcher in baseball in 1968, St. Louis Cardinals ace Bob Gibson, had been another Kennedy backer. After the senator's death, Gibson put together one of the most impressive stretches in the history of the sport. "I really can't say, in retrospect, whether Robert Kennedy's assassination is what got me going or not," Gibson later wrote in his memoir. "Without a doubt, it was an angry point in American history for black people—Dr. King's killing had jolted me; Kennedy's infuriated me—and without a doubt, I pitched better angry. I suspect the control of my slider had more to do with it than anything, but I can't completely dismiss the fact that nobody gave me any shit whatsoever for about two months after Bobby Kennedy died."[11]

Perhaps wiser after his mishandled decision to play ball on the day of Martin Luther King's memorial services, baseball commissioner Spike Eckert postponed games in New York City and Washington scheduled for the day of Kennedy's funeral. Despite President Johnson's declaring a national day of mourning, Eckert declared, other games could be played so long as they started after the funeral services had finished. Many players objected.

New York Mets players voted not to play their game against the San Francisco Giants even though forty thousand tickets had been sold for a scheduled Bat Day giveaway. In Cincinnati, Reds pitcher Milt Pappas tried to rally his teammates' support for postponing their game against St. Louis. The players' vote resulted in a 12–12 tie with one abstention, and manager Dave Bristol intervened to secure a 13–12 decision to play. "You guys are wrong," Pappas shouted at his teammates. "I'm telling you you're all wrong."[12]

Reds executive Dick Wagner encountered Pappas before the game. Pappas recalled the incident as follows: "[Wagner] stopped me on the field in front of the St. Louis dugout and started to put his finger on my shoulder as if he were some kind of tough guy. He was one of those short guys who was mad at God for making him short, so he had this enormous chip on his shoulder. I looked him in the eye and said, 'If that finger reaches my shoulder I'm going to break it.' I meant it and he knew it."[13]

Two Houston Astros players refused to play and earned a fine from team general manager Spec Richardson. Columnist Red Smith criticized the penalties: "Among all the mealy-mouthed statements, it remained for Richardson to come up with the nauseating prize. The games would go on, he said, because 'Senator Kennedy would have wanted it that way.'" Robert Kennedy's press secretary sent notes to Pappas, the Mets, and the two Astros, saying, "Please accept my personal admiration for your actions. Senator Kennedy indeed enjoyed competitive sports, but I doubt that he would have put box office receipts ahead of national mourning." Seventy-two hours later, Pappas was traded. The Reds insisted the transaction had nothing to do with the Kennedy situation.[14]

Journalists widely panned baseball's ham-handed handling of another trying time. Many reporters thought that allowing athletes any say in deciding whether to play was further indication of decay in American society. Dick Young, whom Howard Cosell labeled a "right wing cultural illiterate," called for the commissioner's resignation in his syndicated column. "This is the portrait of a commissioner trying to please everyone," Young wrote. "I have funny, old fashioned notions that students should not run universities, inmates should not run asylums, and ball players should not tell owners when they will play." But Red Smith took up for the players, writing, "The refusal of the Mets to play in San Francisco on the day of Robert Kennedy's funeral was one of the few heartening aspects of a week of shame."[15]

The week of Kennedy's death, folk-rock duo Simon and Garfunkel's "Mrs. Robinson" reached number one on the American pop charts, spurred by the popularity of the movie *The Graduate*, in which it appeared. One of the song's more memorable lines asked, "Where have you gone, Joe DiMaggio, a nation turns its lonely eyes to you." When Paul Simon and Mickey Mantle later appeared on the *Dick Cavett Show* together, Mantle asked during a commercial break, "How come you wrote that song about DiMaggio? Why didn't you write it about me?" Simon, a lifelong Mantle fan, once told a reporter, "Mantle was my guy. Mantle was about the promise of youth." But, as Simon explained to Mantle, DiMaggio's name fit the meter of the song. "It's about syllables, Mick," Simon said. "It's about how many beats there are."[16]

Mantle had arrived in New York in 1951 as the most heralded prospect in baseball history and the heir apparent to DiMaggio as the face of the Yankees. During Game Two of that year's World Series against the New York Giants, Willie Mays hit a soft fly ball to right center field. Mantle chased the ball from right field at full speed until DiMaggio called him off at the last moment. As he altered his course to avoid DiMaggio, Mantle took a bad step and wrenched his knee. DiMaggio made the catch, but Mantle was on the ground, moaning in pain. "I was running so fast, my knee just went right out the front of my leg," he told biographer Jane Leavy. "Shit my pants." DiMaggio leaned down to tell the young right fielder that the stretcher was on its way, the longest conversation the pair had shared all season.[17]

Mantle recovered from the injury in time for spring training the following year, but he was still limping. Though he would be an above-average runner for most of his career, he never regained the dazzling speed of his early youth. Mantle would retire with some of the greatest statistics in baseball history—536 home runs and 1,509 runs batted in. His appetite for booze and women was nearly as legendary as his on-field productivity. But in accordance with the unspoken rules of sports journalism that were becoming a relic of a vanishing

Mickey Mantle *arrived in New York as the heir apparent to Joe DiMaggio's iconic role as the Yankees center fielder. Mantle's knee injury suffered at the end of his rookie season robbed him of some of his speed, but he won seven World Series and three MVP awards in a career that defined an era of American sports for many fans.*

era by the late '60s, rumors of his off-field habits tended to stay out of the newspapers. In 1968 Mantle was only a shell of the player he had been in his prime. He showed occasional flashes of the old Mick—a five-for-five game on Memorial Day, with two home runs and five RBIs, for example—but by midsummer his career batting average had slipped below .300. It would remain there for the rest of what would be his final season.

The once-dominant Yankees franchise, which had won twenty-nine pennants in forty-four years since 1921, had seen its fortunes fall alongside Mantle's slow decline. The team had not won an American League title since Columbia Broadcasting Systems bought the team in 1964. Arthur Daley lamented the corporatization of the Bronx Bombers in his syndicated column. "The carpetbaggers and the quick-buck men have taken over a game that once had true sportsmen at the controls," he wrote. "Now the Yankees are owned by a corporation that is gaited exclusively to producing entertainment. The baseball phase of it is incidental. If this deal is a portent of the future, it is an ominous one. The dollar sign is beginning to obscure the standings of the teams."[18]

As Mantle hobbled into the sunset in the summer of '68, baseball fans were losing an American sports icon who embodied an era of baseball appealing to those who longed for a simpler and happier time. The distinction between the romanticized past and the troubled present would become starker when thousands of demonstrators, most of them young, white, middle-class, and well educated, took to Chicago streets the week of the Democratic National Convention. They protested the Vietnam War and challenged a social and political order that they believed perpetuated racism and inequality in the United States. These activists rejected not only the establishment candidate, Hubert Humphrey, but also the peace candidates and the entire two-party political system in America.

A group calling itself the Yippies (Youth International Party) was one of the major organizers of the Chicago protests. Founded by anarchist Abbie Hoffman and former Cincinnati newspaper reporter Jerry Rubin in Hoffman's Lower East Side apartment on New Year's Eve 1967, the party combined a movement, a slogan, and a general antiauthoritarian attitude. Weeks later, the Yippies circulated a manifesto in the underground press. "All . . . rebels, youth spirits, rock minstrels, truth seekers, peacock freaks, poets, barricade jumpers, dancers, lovers and artists" were invited to come to Chicago during the Democratic Convention in August, and they were urged to bring "blankets, tents, draft cards, body paint, Mrs. Leary's cow, food to share, music, eager skin and happiness." Earlier that year, Hoffman and some friends had caused a stir during a public tour of the New York Stock Exchange when they hurled a pile of one-dollar bills onto the exchange floor from an observation balcony and watched the brokers scurry around in pursuit of the cash. The Yippies wanted that kind of visual spectacle in Chicago, but on a bigger stage and in front of the national media. In planning a presence at the convention, the Yippies built on the efforts of the Mobilization Committee to End the War in Vietnam. During that group's protest at the Pentagon, a few of the demonstrators had unsuccessfully attempted to levitate the building through meditation and chanting.[19]

Chicago had been preparing for possible disturbances for months. City police were ready to maintain order in the face of the planned demonstrations, which they believed embodied everything that was wrong in America, including criminals coddled by courts and the marginalization of the white working class. To Mayor Daley the protesters represented not just a general threat to the American social structure, but a personal threat to his political machine. Daley had a formidable force at his disposal. Six thousand National Guardsmen would reinforce 12,000 Chicago police, and an additional 7,500 army troops would be waiting in the suburbs armed with rifles, bazookas, and flame-throwers. The FBI was monitoring organizers of the rallies, and as many as one in six protesters were actually government agents. "Never before had so many feared so much from so few," noted Chicago columnist Mike Royko.[20]

On the first day of the convention, Yippie leaders advised protesters to leave Lincoln Park peacefully by the 11:00 p.m. curfew. But many chose to stand their ground. As the curfew neared, some of the demonstrators constructed a barricade of park benches, tree branches, and other assorted debris. Others scampered outside the park to disrupt traffic, overturn trash cans, and throw rocks and bottles. When police tried to stop the vandals, violence ensued as TV cameras and newspaper photographers documented the trouble. Law enforcement officers who thought that the journalists betrayed a liberal bias then attacked the journalists. Most of the occupants of the park dispersed peacefully, but a thousand stood their ground behind their makeshift wall.

When a police car rammed through the barrier after midnight, demonstrators pelted it with rocks and bottles, shattering the windows. Three hundred officers in gas masks fired smoke grenades and tear gas as gagging protesters scurried into the streets. The resulting brawl between cops and the youthful assemblage lasted most of the night, with police attacking indiscriminately. A carbine-wielding cop even fractured the skull of a minister in a clerical collar. Fifteen police were injured in the melee, medics affiliated with protest organizers treated eighty activists for serious scalp wounds, and others sought treatment in local hospitals. After calm was restored, cops slashed tires, broke windows, and snapped antennae of cars in a nearby parking lot, taking particular aim at those with McCarthy bumper stickers.

The next morning the Yippies held a press conference, and national news organizations including CBS, ABC, and *Newsweek* sent letters to Mayor Daley objecting to the aggressive behavior of the police. The *Tribune* voiced support for journalists but equivocally claimed, "Some of the newsmen looked like hippies and perhaps they refused to obey police orders to move. If so the police perhaps were justified in using force."[21]

That night a portion of the Lincoln Park congregation moved south to Grant Park, within view of TV cameras in front of the nearby Conrad Hilton Hotel, headquarters for the Democratic Party and the press. It was the only location outside of the International Amphitheater, site of the convention, where Daley allowed TV crews to set up mobile units. An electrical workers' strike

Military police in Chicago *confront a demonstrator outside the Conrad Hilton,
the headquarters hotel for the Democratic National Convention. (AP Photos/RHS)*

prevented live feeds from anywhere except the convention itself. However,
cameramen recorded the violent images, which would be shown periodically
on national television networks' prime-time convention coverage.

The crowds in Grant Park remained peaceful and included many
McCarthy and Kennedy delegates returning from the convention. Unwilling
to risk additional bloodshed in view of the cameras, law enforcement allowed
the demonstrators to remain overnight. Order prevailed even when National
Guard troops emerged in barbed wire–topped Jeeps to relieve the exhausted
cops. But back in Lincoln Park, hundreds had gathered at the foot of a large
cross set up by a group of clergymen. After midnight, police began a tear gas
assault on the group. A special gas-spewing garbage truck sent the crowd
running, at which point law enforcement agents in gas masks again went after
the protesters, cracking several skulls and knocking a minister unconscious.

NBC's *Today* show aired a story the next morning informing viewers that
Chicago police had been beating journalists, "not in spite of the fact they were
newsmen but because of it." NBC commentator Chet Huntley later reported,
"Chicago police are going out of their way to injure newsmen, and prevent

them from filming or gathering information on what is going on. The news profession in this city is now under assault by the Chicago police."[22]

That evening ten thousand people gathered at Grant Park in preparation for a march on the convention site. The Democrats would nominate Hubert Humphrey as their candidate for president later that night, and law enforcement wanted to reduce the chance for disturbances any way they could. A teenager lowered the American flag from a flagpole and was beaten by police who were bombarded with rocks, food, bags of urine, and chunks of concrete. As cops were removing the young man, a group of protesters raised a red T-shirt on the flagpole, drawing further ire from police. As the throng began to mobilize, the National Guard entered the park armed with M-1 rifles, grenade launchers, gas dispensers, bayonets, and machine guns.

The troops took a defensive position and maintained order for over an hour. But the situation deteriorated when thousands of demonstrators again started to move from the park toward the convention hall. Within sight of the TV cameras outside the Hilton, cops began beating protesters and bystanders in what one reporter labeled a "sadistic romp." The dissidents responded by attacking police. Away from the front lines, the mob chanted, "The whole world is watching." From his room in the Hilton, author Norman Mailer observed the clash below. "The police attacked . . . like a scythe through grass," he wrote, "lines of twenty and thirty policemen striking out in an arc, their clubs beating, demonstrators fleeing. Seen from overhead, from the nineteenth floor, it was like wind blowing dust, or the edge of waves riding foam on the shore."[23]

Some ninety million viewers watched live television shots from inside the convention hall that were beginning to resemble the action in the streets. Helmeted, baton-wielding police periodically stormed the convention floor and dragged out delegates who objected to excessive checking of their credentials. After striking CBS's Mike Wallace, a security guard insisted, "[He] hit me first." Reporter Dan Rather was roughed up by guards as he tried to interview an ejected Georgia delegate. "I'm sorry to be out of breath," Rather huffed on air to Walter Cronkite, "but somebody belted me in the stomach."

Cronkite noted, "I think we've got a bunch of thugs here, Dan, if I may be permitted to say so."[24]

Writers Gore Vidal and William F. Buckley nearly came to on-air fisticuffs during one of their nightly debates on ABC television's convention-week programming. Vidal, a leftist, called the noted conservative a "crypto-Nazi," causing Buckley to snarl, "Now listen, you queer! Stop calling me a crypto-Nazi, or I'll sock you in your goddamn face and you'll stay plastered." The debates

During a nominating speech at the Democratic National Convention, Illinois delegates jeer Sen. Abraham Ribicoff when the senator blasted the "Gestapo tactics" of Chicago police. (Library of Congress.)

were intended to be contentious ratings grabbers. But the sparks between the two exceeded all expectations and complemented the combative tone in Chicago that week.[25]

Connecticut senator Abraham Ribicoff took the stage at the convention ostensibly to make a nomination speech, but he drew the ire of Mayor Daley when he criticized the "Gestapo" tactics of Chicago law enforcement. All week Daley had tried to paint protesters as "outside agitators," and he had no patience for anyone who wanted to treat the protests as a legitimate part of the American political process. The mayor sat at the front of the convention with the Illinois delegation. Television microphones did not pick up his words, but even amateur lip readers had no difficulty determining that he shouted, "Fuck you, you Jew son of a bitch, you lousy motherfucker, go home."[26]

After surviving Ted Kennedy supporters' last-minute backroom push to grab the nomination for the youngest brother of Bobby and Jack, Humphrey was nominated on the first ballot. Late that night, cops stormed Gene McCarthy staff headquarters on the fifteenth floor of the Hilton; officers had received word that an object had been thrown from that level. Police used a master key to access the rooms and dragged McCarthy staffers from bed to beat them. Daley defended his police force the next morning, calling the protesters "terrorists" and denouncing the television coverage of the demonstrations. He later told reporters, "I think you newsmen missed the point. No one was killed." Nearly seven hundred dissidents had been arrested that week. Hundreds of people were injured, including nearly three dozen journalists and several dozen police.[27]

Playwright Arthur Miller, a McCarthy delegate from Connecticut, analyzed his convention experience in a piece for the *New York Times Magazine*. "There had to be violence for many reasons," he wrote, "but one fundamental cause was the two opposite ideas of politics in this Democratic party. The professionals—the ordinary senator, congressman, state committeeman, mayor, officeholder—see politics as a sort of game in which you win sometimes and sometimes you lose. Issues are not something you feel, like morality, like good and evil, but something you succeed or fail to make use of. To these men an issue is a segment of public opinion which you either capitalize on or attempt to assuage according to the present interests of the party. To the amateurs—the McCarthy people and some of the Kennedy adherents—an issue is first of all moral and embodies a vision of the country, even of man, and is not a counter in a game." [28]

Accepting the nomination Thursday night, Humphrey condemned all violence and brutality and called for national unity. The spectacle in Chicago would be an initial setback for the Democratic candidate, as millions of Americans did not like what they saw on their televisions that week. Little blame could be directly attributed to Humphrey. Even so, the violent scenes both inside and outside the convention were distasteful to Americans across the political spectrum, and they became an albatross for Democrats for the remainder of the campaign.

As tension surrounding the presidential election was ratcheting up, the American sports world was in a late-summer lull. Weeks before the start of the World Series, the major-league pennant races were all but decided, and football season had yet to start. In early September, tennis fans at the West Side Tennis Club in Forest Hills, Queens, New York, witnessed a series of firsts. Arthur Ashe, an army lieutenant working as a data processor at the United States Military Academy at West Point, became the first African American man to

Protesters in front of the Atlantic City Convention Hall, site of the Miss America Pageant, Sept. 7, 1968. (AP Photo)

win the most prestigious tennis tournament in America. First contested in 1881 as the US National Championships, it was called the US Open for the first time in 1968, the inaugural year of the "Open Era" of competitive tennis in which amateurs and professionals could compete against each other in major tournaments. Ashe was the first male player of color to win any of the four tennis events that constitute the modern Grand Slam.

Because he was still an amateur, Ashe received no prize money for his win, but his victory at the Open was historic. Even so, the *New York Times* cautioned readers, "Let no one cite Lieut. Arthur Ashe's splendid victory in center court at Forest Hills as evidence of strides in the resolution of the Negro problem in America." Two weeks earlier, Ashe had won the US Amateur and had reminded the press that he would not be allowed to join "seven-eighths" of the tennis clubs where he played tournaments.[29]

While Ashe was slicing through the US Open field, scores of women gathered to protest the Miss America pageant on the boardwalk in Atlantic City, New Jersey. Led by former child actress Robin Morgan, the protesters deposited what they called symbols of feminine oppression and objectification—bras, makeup, mops, cooking pots, high-heeled shoes, copies of *Playboy* and *Cosmopolitan*, and makeup—into a "Freedom Trash Can." They decried the "degrading mindless boob-girlie symbol" that the pageant celebrated and protested "ludicrous 'beauty' standards." Taking a page from the Yippie playbook, the women crowned a live sheep, saying that beauty contests were akin to livestock shows at county fairs. Though the trash can was not actually set aflame, rumors to that end gave rise to the image of the "bra burner" in American political discourse.[30]

The Detroit Tigers had clinched the 1968 American League pennant by mid-September after falling a game short the year before, a season marked by deadly rioting in Detroit. Following World War II, Detroit had experienced a huge economic downturn as defense contracts dried up, businesses moved to the suburbs, and automakers decentralized their manufacturing. Young, affluent white families left the urban center for the suburbs, leaving the city with a net drop in population of some two hundred thousand people during the 1950s. Those who remained lived in a deteriorating city whose police force operated under what Detroit's leading black newspaper, the *Michigan Chronicle*, called a "planned policy of containment and harassment of average negro citizens."[31]

By the early sixties, blight was "creeping like a fungus through many of Detroit's proud old neighborhoods." Urban shoppers paid 20 percent more for groceries than their suburban counterparts, a shrinking tax base sapped the budgets of city schools, and overcrowding contributed to high dropout rates. The auto industry was still employing huge numbers of Detroiters, though whites were nearly seven times more likely to get higher-paying white-collar jobs than blacks were. "The Negroes in Detroit feel that they are part of an occupied country," the president of the city's branch of the NAACP explained in 1965. "The Negroes have no rights which the police have to respect. It would appear that the average policeman looks upon the Negro as being a criminal type." In 1967 only 5 percent of the city's police officers were black, even though African Americans submitted nearly half of the applications for positions in the police department.[32]

That summer, long-simmering frustrations came to a boil. When police raided a black-owned after-hours club in the predawn hours of July 23, 1967, they set off five days of fiery riots. An unusually large crowd had crammed

into the speakeasy at the corner of 12th Street and Clairmount Avenue to cel-
ebrate the return of two soldiers from Vietnam. Following the raid, it took
more than an hour for the cops to summon sufficient transportation for all
the arrestees. In the meantime, the proceedings attracted a bevy of onlook-
ers, some of whom verbally objected to the police officers' rough behavior. A
bottle thrown by a member of the crowd begat more agitation, and by 6:00
a.m. thirty windows had been smashed in the vicinity. By noon there were
eight thousand people in the streets. When a (false) rumor circulated that a
white policeman had bayoneted a young black man, the mood of the crowd
became more menacing. In the early afternoon, firefighters were attacked,
and by 3:30 violence had spread beyond the area police had cordoned off. The
mayor asked Governor Romney to mobilize the National Guard.[33]

Across town, the Tigers were in a tight pennant race, playing the last-place
Yankees in a doubleheader. Detroit mayor Jerome Cavanagh had convinced
most local media not to report the early violence, so much of the crowd knew
nothing about the situation developing three and a half miles away. Smoke
from the fires was visible over the left field stands. Per instructions from WJR
management, however, Tiger radio announcer Ernie Harwell did not mention
it on the air. Word of the trouble spread through the clubhouse between contests. Tigers outfielder Willie Horton, who had grown up in Detroit housing
projects as the youngest of twenty-one children and had become the Tigers'
first African American star, headed straight for the riot zone after the game.
"I didn't even remove my uniform," he later recalled. "I drove over by 12th
Street near the blocks where I had delivered *Michigan Chronicle* newspapers
as a child. It looked like a war zone. I exited my car, climbed on the roof and
started shouting at people until I got their attention. 'Why are you burning
and tearing up the neighborhood you live in?' I asked. I kept asking why are
you doing this, but no one had an answer."[34]

Because it was a Sunday, Detroit police officials had difficulty rounding up
enough troops to restore order. In response to early looting, the police initially
made few arrests, stopping only the people who "flaunted their goods in the
cops' faces or taunted them," according to the *Chronicle*. Any early restraint by
law enforcement soon receded as the violent disruption continued to spread.
Late that night, Governor Romney said of law enforcement's authority to fire
on looters, "Fleeing felons are subject to being shot at." After hours of political gamesmanship with Romney, President Johnson sent five thousand army
paratroopers to the streets of Detroit. Five days later calm had been restored
to the city, but at least forty-three people had died, seven thousand had been
arrested, and two thousand buildings had been burned.[35]

A National Guardsman patrols a Detroit street during the city's riots in July 1967.
(AP Photo/File)

The city's wounds had not yet healed the following summer, but the Tigers' championship run was something of a distraction. Detroit pitcher Jon Warden remembered, "The city of Detroit was still in the worst way. There was no denying that. But we began to feed off each other. Everybody in town began to rally around the team. Soon those of us in uniform began to feel like we were fighting for something bigger than just another ballgame. That somehow an entire city, the future of Detroit, was at stake too."[36]

Tigers pitcher Mickey Lolich explained the situation: "In '68, there were still plenty of people who thought the city was going to burn to the ground. That it was all going to fire up again. I had some friends in the police. They were in the city and had a good feel for what was going on. They told us to please keep winning—that things were smoldering, like how it is before it starts burning all over again. But if we could keep winning then things may not explode like they had the year before." Like many players whose teams wanted to protect them from being drafted into the army, Lolich served in the National Guard. He had missed the start of the season after being called to active duty as the city braced for more riots in the wake of Martin Luther King's murder.[37]

The Tigers leapt to the top of the American League standings early in the 1968 season and remained there all summer. On September 19, Mickey Mantle and the New York Yankees were in town for what would be the future Hall of Famer's final game at Tiger Stadium. In the eighth inning Denny McLain, the Tigers eccentric ace pitcher, stepped off the mound to let Mantle soak up one last ovation from the nine thousand fans in attendance. McLain, who would finish the year with a 31–6 record and a 1.96 earned run average on his way to the American League Cy Young and MVP Awards, called catcher Jim Price to the mound and told him that he planned to give his childhood hero a pitch he could drive. Mantle needed one home run to pass Jimmie Foxx for third place on the all-time list, behind only Babe Ruth and Willie Mays. McLain wanted to be sure that Mantle reached that venerable plateau.

"So the first pitch it was, like, fifty miles per hour and almost on an arc," McLain recalled. "And dummy takes it for strike one. Mantle looks down at Price and said, 'What the fuck was that?' And Price says, 'I dunno.' So Mantle says, 'Is he gonna do it again?' And Price says, 'I dunno.' I throw the next pitch almost the same way, but the pitch slid a little bit and he fouled it off. I'm thinking, 'Oh my God, Jesus, now I got him oh and two.'" McLain then yelled at Mantle, asking him where he wanted the pitch. Mantle "put his hand out about balls high on the outside part of the plate," and McLain delivered the requested pitch. Mantle slammed it into the upper deck just inside the right-field foul pole.[38]

Players in the Tiger dugout all stood and applauded. "I think we all had tears in our eyes," McLain later said, "because Mickey Mantle represented the game of the 1960s right up to the day he retired." The next Yankee to the plate was Joe Pepitone, who pointed to where he would prefer a pitch but did not receive the Mantle treatment. "He threw a ball ninety miles an hour at my head," Pepitone recalled. "I went down. I get up. I look at the dugout. Mickey's got his hand over his mouth laughing his ass off." [39]

Not everyone found the situation amusing, however. Baseball commissioner Spike Eckert sent McLain a letter accusing him of attacking the integrity of the game. A fan in Cincinnati griped to his local newspaper, "Can you imagine old Judge Landis [commissioner from 1920 to 1944] if he had been around? Both Mantle and McLain would have been out of baseball right there. Today's prima donnaish players don't seem to realize how sick the game is." But syndicated columnist Red Smith defended the act, noting, "When a guy has bought 534 drinks in the same saloon, he's entitled to one on the house."[40]

After the game, Mantle told reporters, "I think it was just a straight fastball. It's got to be one of the best thrills I've had in baseball." In the Tigers' locker room, McLain grinned at a flock of reporters and said, "I think you guys think I gave it up on purpose." He acknowledged that Mantle had been his idol growing up. "Still is," he said. "Baseball is going to be sad when he leaves."[41]

Mantle had been taking Butazolidin, known to be harmful to human tissue, to help him stagger through his last season, which came to an end in Fenway Park against the Boston Red Sox two weeks later. Yankees manager Ralph Houk told Mantle that he would remove him early, so Mantle didn't take his Bute that day. After popping out to shortstop in the top of the first, he took the field for the bottom half of the inning, tossed the ball around the infield, and was removed after the first batter was announced. Mantle limped back to the dugout for the final time as twenty-five thousand Sox fans acknowledged a worthy adversary with a standing ovation. At the Yankees' request he would wait until spring training to make his official announcement, but he told the *New York Daily News* that he was through. "I just can't hit anymore," Mantle conceded.[42]

_____

Both the Tigers and the St. Louis Cardinals built big midseason leads in their respective leagues and cruised to the World Series. The Cardinals were seeking to cement their status as one of the great teams of the era, having won the Series in 1964 and 1967. In a season that would be known to history as the "year of the pitcher," none was more dominant than Bob Gibson, one of the greatest athletes ever to pitch in the major leagues. Gibson's 1968 season was one of the most impressive in the history of the sport. He won 22 games and lost 9, with a 1.12 earned run average. He had 13 shutouts, 28 complete games, and 268 strikeouts on his way to the National League Cy Young and Most Valuable Player Awards. Gibson reached his pinnacle in 1968, but he had already enjoyed a long and accomplished athletic career.

The youngest of seven children, Gibson grew up in the housing projects of Omaha, Nebraska. Though he suffered through a number of childhood health issues, including rickets, pneumonia, and asthma, he became a star athlete in high school. Gibson had wanted to play basketball at Indiana University, but he was told that the team had already filled its quota of one black player. Gibson instead became the first African American to play basketball for Creighton University, setting the school's career scoring record before signing with both the Cardinals and the Harlem Globetrotters. He played briefly with the Globetrotters before deciding to focus on baseball, and he quickly became one of the most intimidating hurlers in the game.

"The basis of intimidation, as I practiced it, was mystery," Gibson explained. "I wanted the hitter to know nothing about me—about my wife, my children, my religion, my politics, my hobbies, my tastes, my feelings, nothing. I figured the more they knew about me, the more they knew what I might do in a certain situation. That was why, in large part, I never talked to players on other teams. That was why I never apologized for hitting anybody. That was why I seemed like an asshole to so many people." Part of Gibson's intimidation was related to his race and the social context in which he was playing. "There's no way to gloss over the fact that racial perception contributed a great deal to my reputation," he said. "I pitched in a period of civil unrest, of black power and clenched fists and burning buildings and assassinations and riots in the streets. There was a country full of angry black people in those days, and by extension—and by my demeanor on the mound—I was perceived to be one of them."[43]

The 1968 World Series included seven future Hall of Famers, but in Game One Gibson outshined them all, including Tigers starter Denny McLain, a talented musician who had been playing the organ at the hotel bar the night before. Gibson broke Sandy Koufax's Series record with seventeen strikeouts in a 4–0 shutout of the Tigers in one of the most dominating performances in the history of baseball's greatest stage. After the game, Gibson received a congratulatory phone call from Vice President Humphrey. Richard Nixon referenced the accomplishment at a Long Island campaign stop. "This administration has set a record in striking out for America," Nixon said. "It struck out in peace abroad; it struck out on peace at home; it struck out on stopping the rise in crime, and it struck out in stopping rising prices."[44]

Detroit rebounded with an 8–1 win in Game Two behind pitcher Mickey Lolich, who helped himself with the only home run of his major-league career. The best-of-seven series was then sent to Detroit tied at one. After a 7–3 Cardinals win in Game Three, a rematch of Gibson versus McLain loomed for the following afternoon. The vice president attended Game Four with baseball legend Jackie Robinson, and the crowd of over fifty thousand endured a rain delay of thirty-seven minutes to start the game. During the regular season, umpires decided whether to play in the event of rain. But during the World Series, the decision was up to the commissioner. The players correctly surmised that Eckert was reluctant to postpone a game with a television audience expected to approach thirty million viewers. Fans and journalists criticized

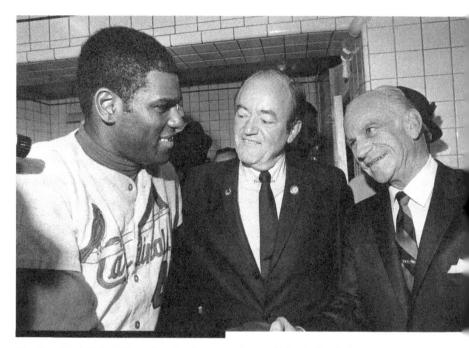

Vice President Hubert Humphrey (center) *congratulates St. Louis Cardinals pitcher Bob Gibson following a 10-1 victory over the Detroit Tigers in Game Four of the 1968 World Series.*

his decision to proceed, particularly after a second rain delay lasted over an hour.

The conditions did not agree with McLain, who recalled in his memoir, "I'm not a mudder, and Game Four was as bad as it gets. When I walked out for the first inning, it was drizzling, and when I threw the first pitch it was coming down in buckets. Actually, the first pitch went OK. It was the second pitch that [Cardinals left fielder Lou] Brock hit into the center field stands four hundred and thirty feet away." St. Louis added a run in the first, then two more in the third on their way to a 10–1 rout. Gibson pitched another gem and knocked a home run, despite being harassed much of the previous night by Tigers fans at the hotel.

———

The Tigers were down three games to one, a hole from which only two teams had ever escaped to win a World Series. For Game Five, the last game of the

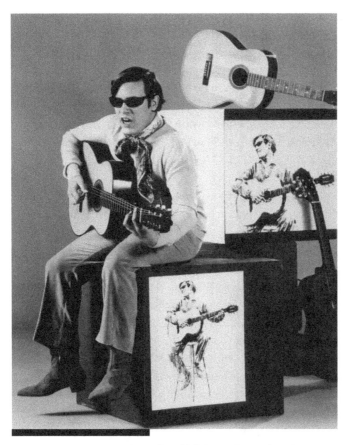

Puerto Rican-born pop singer Jose Feliciano, *pictured here in a promotional image for a 1969 television special, appalled many baseball fans with his unorthodox rendition of the national anthem before Game Five of the 1968 World Series.*

series in Detroit, Tigers broadcaster Ernie Harwell arranged for blind Puerto Rican–born singer Jose Feliciano, whose version of The Doors' "Light My Fire" had sold a million copies that summer, to sing the pregame national anthem. Harwell, himself a songwriter of some renown, had it on good authority that the singer was most capable.

"The Star-Spangled Banner" had been periodically performed at baseball games since the Civil War. However, it was first heard at the World Series in 1918, amidst a period of patriotic fervor as World War I was winding down and domestic civil discontent was high. A military band played a quick rendition of the song during the seventh-inning stretch of Game One between the Cubs and the Red Sox that year. The result was a "patriotic outburst from the crowd," whose modest size journalists attributed to the war's deflationary effect on American enthusiasm for sports. Hometown Chicago fans had little else to cheer about as Babe Ruth, pitching for the visiting Boston Red Sox, shut out the Cubs that day. When the series moved to Boston, the Sox included the song in a pregame ceremony honoring wounded warriors in attendance. An act of Congress declared "The Star-Spangled Banner" the national anthem in 1931, and many teams made it a regular presence at major-league ballparks during World War II.[45]

By 1968, the national anthem was an accepted part of pregame festivities. But that year patriotic rituals took on heightened significance and carried the potential for cultural and political divisiveness. Accompanied onto the field by his guide dog Trudy, Feliciano performed a heartfelt but atypical rendition while playing a Latin-style classical guitar. When the song ended, much of the crowd in Tiger Stadium sat in stunned silence. Some fans murmured expressions of bewilderment and clapped politely, while many booed emphatically. Reactions from the millions of television viewers were similarly mixed, though the negative opinions tended to be the most vocalized. Complaints flooded the phone lines of NBC's affiliates and local newspapers. A St. Louis television station fielded two hundred calls within minutes. Tiger Stadium received two thousand complaints in an hour, and the story made the front page of newspapers in Detroit, St. Louis, New York, and Los Angeles.[46]

Denny McLain explained, "It was a long version of the song and at that point in time, singers weren't supposed to give their own interpretations. This was the height of the Vietnam War and the protest movement. The National Guard was all over the field in a patriotic display, and here's this blind Latino supposedly 'butchering' the anthem. It was perhaps viewed as sacrilegious, rather than an impressive artistic interpretation."[47]

The Tigers' Game Five starting pitcher, Mickey Lolich, gave up three runs in the first inning. He blamed his mistakes on Feliciano, stating, "[His performance had me] so upset that I couldn't straighten myself out." After the rough start, Lolich held the Cardinals scoreless, and Al Kaline's two-run single to right field put Detroit ahead to stay in the bottom of the seventh. The Tigers staved off elimination, but the anthem nearly overshadowed the game in the press.[48]

Harwell later defended his recommendation of Feliciano: "I picked him because he's one of the outstanding singers in America today. I had heard from people in music whose opinion I respect that he had an interesting version of the national anthem. I feel a fellow has a right to sing any way he can sing it." Others disagreed. "I got sick," one reader wrote to the *Detroit Free Press*. Another groused, "No matter how wrong our country might seem to some people, it did not deserve the horrible rock-n-roll rendition given the anthem . . . It makes one ashamed." Governor Romney was "disappointed" by the performance, and a listener told Harwell, "Anybody who'd let that long-hair hippie ruin our Star-Spangled Banner has got to be a Communist."[49]

A group of Vietnam War veterans sent a letter to the *Sporting News* expressing their disgust. "Some of us have seen people die in Vietnam, soldiers singing parts of the National Anthem as they gave their lives for our country," the veterans wrote. "Then to be in a hospital with injuries and illnesses we got in service and to hear the Anthem sung in such a dishonorable way! If some of us had been in the color guard, we would have walked off the field. This was a disgrace to patriotism, to men in the service and to baseball."[50]

Feliciano, who had been raised in East Harlem, could not understand the negative reaction that included calls for him to be "deported" to Puerto Rico. "I wanted to contribute something to the country, to express my gratification for what it has done for me," he said. "I love this country. When anyone knocks it, I'm the first to defend it." Despite the negative reaction, plenty of people loved the song. RCA rushed out a single, which soon cracked the Top 50.[51]

Pitching on two days' rest in Game Six, Denny McLain stifled the St. Louis offense, and the Tigers rode a ten-run third inning to a 13–1 win, setting up a winner-take-all seventh game. In the series finale Bob Gibson had a solid pitching performance negated when Cardinals all-star center fielder Curt Flood, who would finish fourth in National League MVP voting to his teammate Gibson, misjudged a line drive off the bat of Tigers slugger Jim Northrup. Flood then slipped on the damp field when he tried to recover. Northrup ended up with a two-out triple, knocking in Norm Cash and Willie Horton for the game's deciding runs. Mickey Lolich surrendered only one run, on a ninth-inning homer, earning his third complete-game victory of the Series as well as MVP honors. The image of Lolich leaping into the arms of his catcher Bill Freehan after the final out immediately became a part of Detroit's collective sports memory.

Flood took responsibility for his fielding mishap, telling Gibson, "I'm sorry. It was my fault." But Gibson defended his teammate. "If Curt Flood can't catch that ball," Gibson told reporters after the game, "nobody can. I'm certainly not going to stand here and blame the best center fielder in the business. Why couldn't we score any runs off that lefthander? That's the reason we lost." Cardinals right fielder Roger Maris, who would soon announce his retirement from baseball, told Flood, "You're the best damn centerfielder I've ever seen. I'm proud to have played alongside you."[52]

Many fans and writers held Flood responsible for the loss, reassurances from teammates notwithstanding. Flood took his scapegoat status to heart, and the pain remained with him for the rest of his life. "[I can still see] every detail of that situation in my mind," he told a *Los Angeles Times* reporter twenty-five years later. "It was unquestionably the dimmest, darkest day of my baseball career." [53]

A jubilant crowd of 150,000 converged on downtown Detroit for what Tigers broadcaster Ernie Harwell called the "biggest spontaneous celebration in peacetime American history." *Michigan Chronicle* columnist Frank Lett Sr. expressed hope about the larger impact of the Tigers' victory: "The World Series title could be a big factor in cementing race relations in this town and, believe me, there is much to be desired in this area. Sports fans perhaps do more to ease this tension than any of the media, and this includes newspapers, radio and TV combined."[54]

Widespread looting following the Tigers' win complicated any romanticized notion that baseball had provided a permanent solution to the deeper problems the city faced. But Joe Falls, Tigers beat writer for the *Detroit Free Press*, summarized the significance of the series to a city still recovering from the previous year's upheaval. "My town, as you know, had the worst riot in our nation's history in the summer of 1967, and it left scars which may never fully heal. And so, as 1968 dawned and we all started thinking ahead to the hot summer nights in Detroit, the mood of our city was taut. It was apprehensive. It was fearful. . . . But then something started happening in the middle of 1968. You could pull up to a light at the corner of Clairmount and 12th, which was the hub of last year's riot, and the guy in the next car would have his radio turned up: '. . . McLain looks in for the sign, he's set—here's the pitch . . .' It was a year when an entire community, an entire city, was caught up in a wild, wonderful frenzy."[55]

The Tigers' World Series win hardly healed the city's wounds that the previous summer's violence had exposed and aggravated. But it did provide some welcome diversion. Two days after the conclusion of the series, the attention of the sports world turned to Mexico City and the start of the Olympics. Americans looking for distraction from the nation's social and political strain would soon be disappointed.

four
Mexico City

Though the Democratic Convention in Chicago was a greater spectacle, the Republican version held three weeks earlier in Miami Beach was not without its share of drama. Chicago exposed sharp ideological divisions in American society. But as the British journalists who covered the campaign for the *London Times* noted, "The convention at Miami Beach provided a more explicit statement of the American dilemma: the willful divorce of politics from social realities."[1]

Just a few miles away from the convention site, Miami's black ghetto was awash in riot the night before Nixon accepted the Republican nomination. Hundreds of National Guardsmen armed with bayonets joined local police in their effort to secure twenty-five blocks of the city with the aid of tear gas, warning shots fired over rioters' heads , and the order "Get to your homes" shouted through loudspeakers. One man responded, "I ain't got no home." Three locals were shot dead, and dozens were injured in the uprising. But across the causeway on Miami Beach, miles away from the troubles of the mainland, political business proceeded smoothly. Nixon secured his party's nomination on the first ballot with 692 votes, 25 more than he needed for a simple majority.[2]

With the help of former Dixiecrat Strom Thurmond, and promises to oppose aggressive civil rights expansion, Nixon subdued a late surge of support for Ronald Reagan among southern delegates. Nixon's backers found him to be acceptable enough, but he inspired little overt enthusiasm. An Idaho delegate explained, "I'm not looking for much, just a man who makes a decision. I like Nixon. He wipes his butt the way I do." Among athletes, Bart Starr and Wilt Chamberlain were the most prominent Nixon supporters. That summer Chamberlain backed the Republican candidate, saying, "I will support him for President because when he talks about the problems of the ghetto he makes more sense than any other candidate. To me, Nixon stands for independence—not dependence. He has programs for the black man to become a first-class citizen with an even chance to compete."[3]

Accepting the nomination, Nixon painted a grim picture of the country. "As we look at America, we see cities enveloped in smoke and flame," he said. "We hear sirens in the night. We see Americans dying on distant battlefields abroad. We see Americans hating each other; fighting each other; killing each other at home. As we see and hear these things, millions of Americans cry out in anguish." Nixon called on "the great majority of Americans, the forgotten Americans—the non-shouters, the non-demonstrators"—to help him "restore order" to the nation domestically and to "restore respect for the United States of America" abroad. Finally, he declared, "The long dark night for America is about to end."[4]

By Labor Day, Nixon had established a comfortable lead over Humphrey and Wallace, with polls showing that the Republican nominee would win a three-way vote 43–31–19. Support for Humphrey was flagging, and by the end of the month it appeared that Wallace might even overtake him in second place. The Humphrey campaign was light on cash and short on organization. Their candidate was stuck politically between liberal Democrats dissatisfied with their party's nominee and a sitting president who still wielded plenty of personal power and influence over rank-and-file party leaders.[5]

Meanwhile, in Mexico City, Mexican officials had plenty of reasons for concern in the weeks before the October start of the Olympic Games. "Never has an approaching Olympics been beset by more immediate and potential problems than Mexico City—altitude, racial and political boycotts, riots, red tape, delays," John Underwood wrote in *Sports Illustrated*.[6] In addition to the altitude (over seven thousand feet above sea level) and the civil strife that had plagued the Mexican capital for much of the summer, questions remained about the venues and infrastructure. These would prove to be the least of anyone's trouble.

Professional athletes were strictly forbidden to compete at the Olympics, but the Games had become big business. While Japan had spent $2.7 billion in preparation for the 1964 Games in Tokyo, Mexico had pledged only $176 million. "We are not sure we can guarantee the organization of these games," a Mexican delegate admitted following the Tokyo Olympics. "The weather will be nice, though." Reporters describing the construction process in Mexico returned to old stereotypes of Mexican laziness and disorganization. As to concerns about the altitude, International Olympic Committee president Avery Brundage said, "The Olympic Games belong to all the world, not just the part of it at sea level."[7]

Student-led civil unrest that had spread across much of the world in 1968 reached Mexico City that summer. Between July 23 and August 10, nearly fifty student rallies promoting political and social reform were held in and around Mexico City. For a government trying to polish its image in preparation for the global spotlight, the demonstrations were a serious problem. On August 13, 150,000 protesting students paraded through downtown Mexico City. Two weeks later 200,000 marched on the National Palace, which was vandalized with spray paint. After most of the protesters had gone home, a few thousand lingered. While the police had failed to materialize during the main protest, they arrived to chase away the stragglers, many of whom were armed with makeshift weapons. Violence ensued, leaving four students dead. Mexican president Gustavo Diaz Ordaz addressed the nation and promised to use "all legal means within [his] reach" to maintain order for the Olympics, presumably with the help of riot gear he had been ordering from the United States since May.[8]

One of the protesters' aims was to publicize the needs of the Mexican poor in light of comparatively large government expenditure on the upcoming Games. As one student explained, "The Olympics are the Government's problem, not ours. It is the Government that is going to sabotage the Olympics by creating a climate of repression in this city. The more the Government uses forces the more it is going to have problems." *Sports Illustrated* noted similarities between "Mexico's smoldering young activists" and the American students who had been protesting on campuses from New York to California that year. "Some are true idealists, and some are what Daniel J. Boorstin has termed the New Barbarians. . . . The rioters are clearly anxious to do their thing in front of plenty of witnesses."[9]

The US ambassador to Mexico wired Washington on October 1 to report that tensions were easing in the Mexican capital. This message downplayed the seriousness of the protests, particularly as compared to those in Paris that had nearly toppled the French government that summer. But the next day, around 5:00 p.m., some five thousand students assembled at the Plaza de las Tres Culturas, named for its proximity to Aztec ruins, a colonial church, and a modern foreign ministry building. Plans to demonstrate at a nearby school were abruptly canceled due to the reported presence of troops there. Instead, the assemblage remained in the plaza and listened to some political speeches.

A thousand troops with fixed bayonets arrived in tanks, jeeps, and armored cars around 6:00 p.m. Soon, two helicopters hovering above fired red and green flares, signaling the troops below to seal off the area. Rooftop sharpshooters opened fire, and soldiers charged the students. "Nobody is certain whether the troops or armed students—of whom there were many—fired first," an American journalist reported. "But within minutes a major fire fight raged. Its intensity reminded some of us of combat in World War II and Vietnam."[10]

Some doubted official reports indicating that students had instigated the violence, particularly given that their weapons of choice tended to be rocks rather than guns. Initially the government insisted that only four students had been killed. But as information emerged over the ensuing weeks and years, as many as 325 deaths were attributed to the incident. Hundreds more had been injured and imprisoned, in some cases for years. Just in time for the start of the Games, the protests had been silenced.

The FBI was monitoring the protests and repression and was aware that individuals purportedly representing a Mexican student group called the Comité Anti-Olimpico de Subversión (CAOS) had met with San Jose State College sociologist Harry Edwards in California. As Edwards later recalled, the students told him that they were prepared to lose lives and were committed to stopping the Olympics by any means necessary. Edwards was sympathetic to their cause, and he issued a supportive public statement tying the experiences of African American athletes to those of the Mexican students.[11]

Edwards had grown up impoverished in East St. Louis, Illinois, often without running water. It was exceedingly rare for anyone from his neighborhood to seek post-secondary education, but Edwards enrolled at Fresno City College, where he set a junior-college discus record and grew to 6'8" and 240 pounds. On the heels of that early success, track-and-field coach Lloyd "Bud" Winter recruited him to transfer to San Jose State. When the school could not find him a black roommate, Edwards was assigned to live in a vacant fraternity house undergoing renovation. Because of his race, the multisport star was excluded from the drama club and from the fraternities his basketball team-mates joined. When Edwards and his black friends started attending a regular

Wednesday night campus dance, the format was changed to country-western and finally canceled altogether. There were only a few dozen students of color on a campus of over twenty thousand, and only six black women. Sociology classes taught Edwards to look more critically at a number of San Jose State's unjust policies and institutions. Perhaps most conspicuously, the school's track-and-field program, known as "Speed City," had become one of the best in the nation and had raised the national profile of the school even as some of its athletes were living in equipment sheds and off-campus basements.

After graduating from San Jose State and earning a master's degree from Cornell, Edwards returned to his alma mater to teach sociology. When he saw that athletes still faced housing issues, Edwards organized a protest to be held at the 1967 season-opening football game against the University of Texas–El Paso. Subsequently, the situation escalated into a major problem for the university. The Hell's Angels motorcycle gang promised to interfere with any protests, and the Black Panthers promised to interfere with the Hell's Angels. Governor Ronald Reagan threatened to send the National Guard to "preserve order" and condemned what he called "the appeasement of lawbreakers." University president Robert Clark met with Edwards and promised to address housing issues, diversity in hiring within the athletics department, and fraternity admission policies if the protest was canceled. But by that time the situation had grown beyond Edwards's control. The president asked Edwards for assurance that he could control the Panthers. Edwards conceded that he could not, and he asked the president if he could control the Hell's Angels.[12]

The game's cancellation was the first in the United States attributed to racial conflict, and Governor Reagan called for Edwards's dismissal. Edwards called Reagan a "petrified pig" and "unfit to govern," and their brief standoff quickly raised Edwards's national profile. He became an instant academic celebrity, speaking to dozens of colleges and universities that year. His sartorial choices helped to further distinguish the increasingly activist Edwards from the staid academic establishment. He often wore a black beret, heavy boots, and a matchbook pinned to his lapel, the latter a visible indication that he was prepared to "burn it down." When Martin Luther King first met Edwards, who by that time had filled out his 6'8" frame and weighed 275 pounds, the minister said, "Whoa, I see why those folks are so scared of you." Edwards developed a series of quotable lines for fascinated journalists, including, "Teaching crackers is like kicking through a steel door with Jell-O boots."[13]

A student of Edwards's, San Jose State's top sprinter Tommie Smith, first raised the possibility of an Olympic boycott while in Tokyo for the World University Games in 1967. A Japanese reporter asked Smith whether "Negroes were now equal to whites in how they were treated" in the United States. When Smith said that they were not, the reporter asked about the possibility of a boycott of the upcoming Olympic Games. "Depending on the situation, you cannot rule out the possibility," Smith replied. [14]

After meeting with dozens of athletes, including Smith, at the Los Angeles Black Youth Conference in late November 1967, Edwards announced his intent to organize a boycott of the 1968 Olympics. "For years we have participated in the Olympic Games, carrying the United States on our backs with our victories, and race relations now are worse than ever," Edwards said. "But it's time for black people to stand up as men and women and refuse to be utilized as performing animals for a little extra dog food. You see, this may be our last opportunity to settle this mess short of violence."[15]

Tommie Smith was born in East Texas, the son of a cotton picker. While still a young boy he moved with his family to California's San Joaquin Valley, where his father worked as a school handyman. Smith explained to *Life* magazine how he had developed from a conservative ROTC student to someone who was willing to risk safety and security to stand up for civil rights. "You leave high school, you come to college and you're on your own, but you can't understand the new pressure," Smith said. "What is it? I'm here in college and I'm a great athlete. What's wrong with me? Just walk outside and you feel it. . . . Sit next to a girl with long blond hair and you feel her tense up and try to move over. Talk to a couple of girls in the cafeteria and see what happens. People are reading papers, and first thing you see the papers drop and eyes peering over."[16]

Smith's friend and teammate Lee Evans was equally instrumental in the development of the early boycott movement. "I began to notice a lot of discriminatory things that I had simply accepted," Evans recalled. "I finally began to realize what was being done to me, how I had been stereotyped as a black athlete. Tom and I receive tons of hate letters calling us black bastards. One professor gave Tom a D in a course when he was doing real good work."[17]

A third key member of the movement was John Carlos, described in a *Sports Illustrated* profile as "a goateed, jive-talking slum kid from Harlem who remembers his neighborhood as a place where kids drank cheap scotch and who believes that at least part of his mission in life is to point up the implications of that fact to the establishment." Carlos had been a top junior swimmer in New York before being told that he would find more opportunity in track and field, given the color of his skin. He attended East Texas State University on a track scholarship and was a confident competitor. "I'll save you niggers a piece of the tape" was a favorite prerace line.[18]

International Olympic Committee president Avery Brundage,
widely accused of harboring racist and anti-Semitic sentiments,
insisted that politics had no place at the Games. Pictured here
in Guadalajara on Oct. 20, 1968, during the Mexico City
Olympics. (AP Photo)

While at East Texas, Carlos told the school newspaper that he had heard white football coaches calling their black players "Nigger," "Nigra," and "Boy." He was told by the athletic department, "You don't like it here, you can leave." He did. On a recruiting visit to coach Winter's house, Carlos requested a Jack Daniels when offered something to drink. "We're all men here, right?" he asked the coach. He received his beverage and signed with San Jose State that day. In addition to the track program, Carlos was attracted to San Jose State because Harry Edwards taught there. He was quickly on board with Edward's movement.[19]

Disapproval of the proposed boycott emerged from various corners. One of the most vocal opponents was octogenarian IOC chair Avery Brundage, a self-made millionaire and former Olympic athlete, who called it a "very bad mistake." As chair of the USOC prior to the 1936 Games in Berlin, Brundage had gone to Germany on a "fact finding mission." He wanted to knowledgably respond to the American Athletic Union's calls for a boycott of the Games as a statement of opposition to the Nazi regime. The Nazis rolled out the red carpet for Brundage, and he had a fine time in Germany, even proudly telling some of his Nazi hosts that his Chicago athletic club did not allow Jews to be members. Upon returning to the States, Brundage reported that there was no need for any more discussion of boycotts. He later received assurance that his construction firm would be hired to help build the German embassy in Washington.[20]

In response to the continuing discussion of boycotting the '68 Olympics, San Jose track coach Bud Winter said, "I have worked with the black man and I understand his problems, but boycotting just is not the way to solve them. Smith and Evans are two of the greatest Negro athletes in history. I pray that the United States can clear up problems of racial equality . . . so that they will never have to be confronted with such drastic action. . . . I am appalled Negro athletes have been driven so far as to consider boycotting a movement that epitomizes the very thing for which they are fighting."[21]

Jesse Owens, an African American and the winner of four gold medals at Hitler's 1936 Berlin Games, said, "I deplore the use of the Olympic Games by certain people for political aggrandizement. There is no place in the athletic world for politics." Joe Louis echoed the sentiment: "Maybe [black athletes] don't have equal opportunity in America, but they're gaining it every day and that's something you should realize. Things are improving. If they were going backward it would be different." Hate mail from across the country found its way to leaders and advocates of the protest, including Smith and Evans, calling them "animals," "niggers," "agitating militants," and "jigaboo so-called athletes."[22]

Some members of the black press also joined the chorus of criticism. A. S. "Doc" Young of the *Chicago Defender* wrote: "If Tommie Smith . . . believes 'I'm nothing but a nigger' when he isn't performing on the track, then he is 'nothing but a nigger.' When one considers that millions of American Negroes have withstood the worst of Southern bigotry without ever being reduced to the acceptance of the state, what is Tommie Smith crying so much about? I have nothing but contempt for people who complain because we don't have enough heroes but who spend their time trying to destroy the showcases for which heroes are produced and displayed. The charge that 'America is as racist as South Africa' is the most extravagant lie in our time."[23]

In conjunction with the proposed boycott, Edwards formed the Olympic Project for Human Rights and circulated an informational booklet among US athletes. "We must no longer allow this country to *use* . . . a few 'Negroes' to point out to the world how much progress she has made in solving her racial problems when the oppression of Afro-Americans is greater than it ever was," the manifesto declared. "We must no longer allow the Sports World to pat itself on the back as a citadel of racial justice when the racial injustices of the sports industry are infamously legendary. . . . Any black person who allows himself to be used in the above manner is not only a chump—because he allows himself to be used against his own interest—but he is a traitor to his race. He is secondly, and most importantly, a traitor to his country because he allows racist whites the luxury of resting assured that those black people in the ghettos are there because that is where they want to be. . . . So we ask why should we run in Mexico only to crawl home?"[24]

With Martin Luther King and other civil rights leaders at his side at the Americana Hotel in New York City, Edwards issued a list of demands on behalf of the OPHR on December 14, 1967. The organization called for the exclusion of white-supremacist South Africa and Southern Rhodesia from the Olympics; the integration of the United States Olympic Committee; the addition of at least two black coaches to the men's track team; and the return of Muhammad Ali's championship titles. Edwards also expressed hope that the "devout anti-Semitic and anti-Negro personality Avery Brundage" would be replaced as IOC head.

Brundage owned Montecito Country Club in California, and a report in *Ebony* magazine alleged that he had once said that he would sell the country club "before letting niggers and kikes" become members. Brundage denied the report, but he did say, "If the members chose to accept only red-haired barbers for members, I think it's their right." In response to the OPHR's demands, Brundage called Edwards an "unknown negro agitator" and condemned the group as "an ignorant and misguided . . . attack on the Olympic movement." He said that politics did not belong at the Olympics, "the one international affair for Negroes, Jews, and Communists," adding, "They're all equal on the field of competition. This is a fundamental principle of the Olympics that there be no discrimination."[25]

The OPHR gained early momentum with a successful boycott of the New York Athletic Club meet in February 1968, the first track event to be held in the new Madison Square Garden. In an era when amateur track and field was still a big deal, the meet sponsored by the all-white NYAC was among the most prestigious in the nation and was televised nationally. Entire collegiate teams refused to participate, and only nine black runners attended. Five of them were from UTEP, a school that only two years earlier had won the NCAA men's basketball championship with an all-black team by defeating an all-white squad from the University of Kentucky. O. J. Simpson, who would win the Heisman Trophy as a running back for Southern Cal later that year but was also a top sprinter at USC, skipped the meet. Rather than voice support for the boycott, Simpson claimed that he could not fit the event into his training schedule.

UCLA star Lew Alcindor, arguably the greatest college basketball player in history, gave the protest movement some added visibility when he appeared on NBC's *Today* show that summer and discussed his involvement. Alcindor and the UCLA Bruins had won the NCAA championship that spring, avenging their only loss of the season, to the University of Houston, along the way. The Cougars had won "the Game of the Century" in the Houston Astrodome in January, the first regular-season prime-time college basketball game to be televised nationally. But UCLA prevailed in the rematch at the NCAA semi-finals on its way to a fourth national championship in five years.

On the *Today* show, Alcindor explained to host Joe Garagiola, a former major-league baseball player, why he would not be attending the US Olympic Trials that summer. "Yeah, I live here," Alcindor said, "but it's not really my country."

"Well, then there's only one solution," Garagiola replied, "maybe you should move."

Alcindor, who would change his name to Kareem Abdul-Jabbar in 1971 after winning an NBA championship with the Milwaukee Bucks, later clarified his statement. "What I was trying to get across was that until things are on an equitable basis this is not my country," he explained. "We have been a racist nation with first class citizens and my decision not to go to the Olympics is my way of getting the message across."[26]

The movement also found support in some unlikely places, including the Harvard rowing team. After securing a spot in the Olympics with their win at the Olympic Trials, the Harvard crew offered to support Edwards's protest. The rowers drafted a statement backing the OPHR, and Edwards said it was "beautiful to see some white cats willing to admit they [had] a problem and looking to take some action to educate their own." But United States Rowing officials were unimpressed. They subsequently managed to get seven of the nine Harvard crewmen to sign a pledge swearing off "any demonstration of support for any disadvantaged people in the United States." Anyone who supported the movement risked adverse consequences. In spearheading the campaign, Edwards had faced death threats and was convinced FBI agents were following him. That summer he was evicted from his home, his landlady telling him he was "too much trouble" when his apartment was burglarized and two mutilated dogs were left on his step.[27]

Despite lofty language spouted in the name of OPHR, the group was not fully inclusive, and it did not allow women to participate in the movement on equal footing with men. Wyomia Tyus, who would become the first sprinter to win one-hundred-meter gold in consecutive Olympics, was offended when the leaders of the protest movement treated women as mindless second-class citizens. Coverage of female Olympians in the sports press seemed to reinforce this message.

In describing some of the promising performances by women at the Olympic Trials, *Sports Illustrated* ran a story by Bob Ottum titled "Dolls on the Move to Mexico." Therein, one coach reported "a great influx of pretty young things coming into the sport." Ottum described one runner as "a dainty little thing" and observed, "[I've seen] a great many more girls who look great in these warm-up suits, almost as if they were modeling them for heaven sakes, instead of just keeping their muscles warm." According to the article, the two-hundred-meter event was "that crusher in which a girl must forget everything pretty and just plain run." One spectator, who described himself as a "track nut and announcer," explained, "The girls are finding that there can be a certain air of glamour in all this. For one thing, running does great things for the legs. It makes them shapelier." A track statistician noted, "If you get them running early, the girls can see that they are going to get a lot of attention, and they get to meet a lot of boys that way—not just one or two, like they might otherwise. And the boys get to see them."[28]

Many black athletes were not in favor of an Olympic boycott. Ralph Boston, the defending Olympic champion long jumper, said, "What boycott? I've put too much time and effort into track and field to give it up. If I felt there was sufficient reason I would boycott, but I don't even know what the reason is. At least Negroes have this much: we can compete in amateur sports and we can represent ourselves and then the country." Sprinter Charlie Greene said, "It comes down to [whether] you're an American or if you're not. I'm an American, and I'm going to run." Jesse Owens supported those who planned to run, saying, "We shattered this so-called Aryan supremacy [in 1936] by our own supremacy and by standing and saluting the American flag. I feel that the deeds of an individual are far more potent than a boycott. There is no politics or racial prejudice in the Olympics. I believe you contribute more by entering than by staying out."[29]

Edwards had tried to maintain the façade of unity, but as more athletes spoke out against the proposed protest, he was forced to acknowledge in late August that the boycott was off. But there were still plenty of rumblings regarding possible demonstrations and protests by the athletes during the Games. A week before departing for Mexico City, the team gathered in Denver. Lee Evans told other black athletes, "We can't go down there without deciding something." Sprinter Larry James explained, "It boiled down to a clash between the goal—doing good for all mankind—and the gold—the individual self-interest. There was, shall we say, counseling back and forth to sort out the two."[30]

Tommie Smith told the group, "I have no hate for people who can't make a gesture, whatever the reason. But I have to preserve the honor of Tommie Smith. I'm an American until I die, and to me that means I have to do something." But the challenge was figuring out what that something was. There were suggestions of armbands, bare feet, or black socks on the medal stand. Someone had a problem with each of the suggestions until sprinter Mel Ponder lost his patience and yelled, "You motherfuckers! Shut the fuck up!" and left the room.[31]

The opening ceremony in Mexico City celebrated the Olympics' link to an ancient past, emphasizing stability and continuity, and was unblemished by protest. Writing for the *New York Times*, Arthur Daley called it "the ultimate in stagecraft, soul-stirring in its magnificence." The American team came closest to controversy for the way in which it carried its flag in the Parade of Nations. As the assembly of athletes, organized by nation, marched past President Diaz Ordaz, each delegation dipped its flag in acknowledgment of the host country's leader at the reviewing stand. The Americans were the sole exception; their flag bearer, fencer Janice-Lee Romary, continued an American tradition dating to 1908. John Carlos skipped the festivities, which were otherwise conspicuously uneventful, particularly given the expectations and context.[32]

After a quiet first few days of the Games, the men's two-hundred-meter finals loomed as a must-see event. Smith and Carlos each had survived the qualifying rounds, and each had won his semifinal heat in Olympic-record time. In the finals, two hours later, Smith started from lane three. Carlos was just outside him. Both broke cleanly, but Carlos was three meters ahead as they entered the straightaway. With a burst of power, Smith passed Carlos with eighty meters remaining and coasted to the finish line with his arms

American sprinters Tommie Smith (center) and John Carlos (right) *extend their fists in protest of racial injustice in the United States at the Mexico City Olympics, where Smith won gold and Carlos bronze in the 200 meter finals. The silver medalist, Australian Peter Norman, wears a button in solidarity with the protest.*

raised and a smile on his face. The final time, 19.83 seconds, was a world record. Australian Peter Norman slid past Carlos to win silver, but Carlos's third-place finish earned him a spot on the medal stand.

Though recollections would differ as to when and how the athletes crafted their protest plan, most of it was clearly premeditated. Having earlier readied their podium props, including the black dress socks (*Newsweek* called them "pimp socks") they had worn in the race, Smith and Carlos finalized their strategy in the twenty minutes between the race and the medal ceremony. Smith had a pair of black leather gloves. He took the right glove and gave Carlos the left. To memorialize victims of lynching, Carlos wore a set of beads, and Smith sported a black scarf. As they waited for the ceremony to begin, Norman told the Americans that he wanted to support their cause. He procured an OPHR button from one of the Harvard crewmen and pinned it to his warm-up jacket.[33]

Smith and Carlos approached the podium together. Smith was praying, and Carlos was listening for gunshots he feared could be directed at them. They each wore only socks on their feet. As "The Star-Spangled Banner" began, Smith had "never felt such a rush of pride." He and Carlos raised their fists in what the *Los Angeles Times* called "a Nazi-like salute" and bowed their heads. After a moment of stunned silence, "the stadium rocked with boos and catcalls, some of the spectators made the thumbs-down gestures as they would to a Mexican matador preparing for the kill." Though the protest was a simple one, it genuinely shocked and unnerved many white Americans. As Smith later explained, "It was the fist that scared people. Bowing wouldn't have gotten the response the fist did. It was a silent gesture. I never threw a rock."[34]

Smith and Carlos were again booed as they exited the stadium, and the pair responded with raised fists. Carlos issued a statement to the assembled media to give his perspective: "Tommie Smith and John Carlos would like to put in the papers—print what I say or don't print it at all—that white people feel that black people are nothing but animals, something to do a job. We received many boos out there today. White people turned thumbs down on us. We're not lower animals—roaches or ants or rats. If we do the job well, we get a pat on the back or some peanuts. And someone says, 'Good boy.' I've heard boy, boy, boy all through the Olympics. I'd like to tell white people in America and all over the world that if they don't care for the things black people do, then they shouldn't sit in the stands and watch them."[35]

Though the attention paid to the protest eclipsed the actual race, Carlos implied that he had "let" Smith win. "The upper part of my calves were pulling pretty hard," Carlos told the press. "I wanted to see where Tommie was, and if he could win it. If I thought he couldn't have won it, I would have tried harder to take it." He did not intend for Peter Norman to pass him, but he magnanimously conceded, "Frankly, I thought if a white man could run a 200 meter in 20 flat, he deserved to win silver."[36]

ABC did not get Smith on camera to explain the protest until a day later, when Howard Cosell tracked him down at the hotel to which he had moved after his victory. Smith initially hesitated to discuss the incident. Perhaps disingenuously, he questioned the newsworthiness of the previous day's event, telling Cosell, "You'd think I committed murder. All I did was what I've been doing all along, call the attention of the world to the way the blacks are treated in America. There's nothing new about this."

Cosell replied, "It's new when you do it at a world forum. I think you should state what you did and why you did it. Then at least some people might understand." The cajoling was successful, and Smith agreed to join Cosell on the air, giving the reporter a chance to make what he would later humbly describe as "some of the best damned television in the history of the medium."

When the cameras were rolling, Cosell said, "Tell me, Tommie, what did you mean, symbolically, by the bowed head, the shoeless feet, the outstretched fist?"

"The fist to show Black Power, the strength and unity of the black people," Smith replied. "The shoeless feet to show the anguish of black people through all the years. The bowed head because the words of the anthem were not being applied to blacks." Cosell then asked Smith whether he represented all black athletes. "I can say I represented black America," Smith said. "I'm very proud to be a black man. . . . I thought I could represent my people by letting them know I'm proud to be a black man." When Cosell asked whether Smith was proud to be an American, the sprinter replied: "I am proud to be a black American."[37]

The protest received a mixed review from American athletes. Though boxer George Foreman would claim ignorance of his gesture's larger significance, he gained a national following by trotting around the boxing ring waving a miniature American flag after winning heavyweight gold. Most interpreted this act as a response to the "Anti-American" deeds of Smith and Carlos. Foreman, who had grown up poor in Houston, said that the OPHR was "for college kids," asserting, "They live in another world." A US water polo team member called Smith and Carlos's gesture "a disgrace," stating, "In my opinion, an act like that in the medal ceremony defiles the American flag." But members of the women's four-hundred-meter relay team, led by Wyomia Tyus, dedicated their wins to Smith and Carlos.[38]

ABC surely had gotten plenty of bang from the $4.5 million it had shelled out for American broadcast rights to the Games. By comparison, CBS had paid less than $400,000 to broadcast the 1960 Rome Olympics. But Mexico City's time zone allowed ABC to provide unprecedented coverage of the 1968 Games. Given the way events had unfolded that year in the United States, millions of viewers felt they should not miss a live telecast of a major international sports spectacle.

The US Olympic Committee issued a formal apology to the IOC for "the discourtesy displayed by two members of the U.S. team in departing from tradition during a victory ceremony at the Olympic Stadium." But IOC head Avery Brundage, who had missed the two-hundred-meter final to attend the yachting competition in Acapulco, was not satisfied. He responded, "One of the basic principles of the Olympic Games is that politics play no part whatsoever in them. This principle has always been accepted with enthusiasm by all, of course, including the competitors. Yesterday, the U.S. athletes in a victory ceremony deliberately violated the universally accepted principle by using the occasion to advertise domestic political views." The USOC got the message. The group quickly reconvened and issued a new statement announcing that Smith and Carlos had been kicked off the team and evicted from the Olympic Village. But as Red Smith noted, in forcing the banishment, "the badgers multiplied the impact of the protest a hundredfold. They added dignity to the protestants and made boobies of themselves."[39]

Tommie Smith agreed. "We couldn't have done more to publicize our cause than the committee did," he said. "We're very grateful." Even athletes who did not support the protest thought that the reaction to it was heavy-handed. Irish middle-distance runner Noel Carol called the demonstration by Smith and Carlos "foolish and childish" but also said, "The punishment was even more ridiculous. It was too much for too little. It made heroes of them." A Soviet track coach asserted, "It's too bad. They are supposed to [be] free people. It wouldn't happen to us. We don't mix sports and politics."[40]

Howard Cosell came down squarely against the USOC in an October 18 appearance on *ABC Evening News*:

> Doubtless, the preponderant weight of the American public opinion will support the committee, but nothing is solved, really. [The US Olympic Committee] is, in the main, a group of pompous, arrogant, medieval-minded men who regard the Games as a private social preserve for their tiny clique. They view participation in the Games as a privilege, not as a right earned by competition. They say the Games are sports, not politics, something separate and apart

from the realities of life. But the black athlete says he is part of a revolution in America, a revolution designed to produce dignity for the black man, and that he is a human being before he is an athlete. He says his life in America is filled with injustice, that he wants equality everywhere, not just within the arena. He says that he will not be used once every four years on behalf of a group that ignores what happens to him every day of all the years. . . . He says, Don't tell me about the rules. The U.S. doesn't dip its flag in front of the reviewing stand, and that's a rule all other nations follow. He's aware of backlash but says he's had it for four hundred years. And so the Olympic Games for the United States have become a kind of America in microcosm, a country torn apart. Where will it all end? Don't ask the U.S. Olympic Committee. They've been too busy preparing for a VIP cocktail party next Monday night in the lush new Camino Real. Howard Cosell reporting from Mexico City.[41]

The Mexican government told Smith and Carlos that they could remain in the country as tourists, but the constant swarm of reporters hungry for quotes rendered that option unattractive. Coverage of the controversy moved to the front pages of the nation's newspapers alongside reports from Jackie Kennedy's wedding to Greek shipping magnate Aristotle Onassis, a quiet reminder of all that had changed in America in a few short years.

At one point in the banishment process, Carlos, accompanied by "two New York Negro friends dressed in black power costumes with beads," lost his temper with a large flock of reporters waiting for him outside one of the Olympic buildings. "I want to be left alone," Carlos said. "I told you I want to be left alone. If anybody puts another one of those [microphones] in my face I will knock him down and stomp on him." On October 21, Smith and Carlos relinquished their Olympic documents and boarded a California-bound flight. Their Olympic experience was finished, but the public debate over the sprinters' acts of protest, and the USOC's response, was just starting. It seemed that everyone had an opinion.[42]

Democratic vice presidential nominee Edmund Muskie said that the protest "probably should not have been made," but he conceded that it was difficult to say for sure because the men "were given no hearing." Jackie Robinson said that he "admired their pride in their blackness," and he observed, "The Olympic Committee made a grave mistake in suspending them. What they did had nothing to do with shaming this country." But Bob Seagren, the gold medal–winning American pole vaulter, said, "If it wasn't for the United States they wouldn't have been there. I don't think [the protest] was very proper. If they don't like the United States, they can always leave." Jesse Owens again criticized the protest, saying, "These kids are imbued with the idea that there's a great deal of injustice in our nation. In their own way, they were trying to bring out what is wrong in our country. But I told them that the problem certainly belonged in the continental borders of America. Mexico City was the wrong battlefield."[43]

But many black writers placed the protests within a larger struggle for freedom and equality. The black-owned *Pittsburgh Courier* predicted, "When the years have grown dim, the spectacle of Smith and Carlos, dramatizing the American 'dilemma,' will be a folk tale for black grandmothers yet unborn."[44] In the *Michigan Chronicle*, Frank R. Saunders wrote:

> Classifying the black-gloved clinched fist as a political gesture, the Avery Brundage–led IOC demanded the expulsion of the two athletes.
>
> In defining the gesture Smith explained that the black glove simply meant power and unity. This explanation makes the expulsion all the more ambiguous and asinine when one considers that the very basis on which this nation was founded and still stands lies in its power and unity.
>
> As for the politics, anyone with two grains of sense knows that from the time Jesse Owens stunned the Germans by winning four events, the Olympic games have been one of the biggest political struggles the world has ever known, and it has been the exploits of the black athlete that have enabled the United States to come out on top in this struggle.
>
> It seems that White America will never learn that the time for patting the black man on the head for a job well done is past. The black athlete, and the black man in general, is demanding all the rights guaranteed under the Constitution of the United States and one of those rights is freedom of expression.[45]

Most newspapers tended to be more critical. A *Chicago Tribune* editorial called the demonstration "an embarrassment visited upon the country." And Brad Pye Jr., a journalist, editor, sports administrator, and civic leader, captured the views of many socially conservative African Americans when he declared that the sprinters' "Hitler-like salute" was "out of place" at the Olympics.[46] Brent Musburger, writing in the *Chicago American*, an afternoon paper owned by the *Tribune*, went much further. Calling Smith and Carlos "a couple of black-skinned storm troopers," Musburger opined, "[The sprinters have ensured] maximum embarrassment for the country that is picking up the tab for their room and board here in Mexico City. One gets a little tired of having the United States run down by athletes who are enjoying themselves at the expense of their country." He concluded a long diatribe with an ominous warning: "The way things are going, someone better save all of us before it's too late."[47]

In his wrap-up of the Games for ABC, Cosell sounded a different note. "I should bring to you as the Nineteenth Olympiad comes to its close what I take out of this as a fundamental premise: that it is false any longer to pretend that the Olympic Games anymore are sports and not politics, because they have become exactly the latter—politics. And I think that it is time for the International Olympic Committee, with its archaic curmudgeon of a president, Avery Brundage, and the various national Olympic committees, including our own, to take a look at themselves, and to seek to bring the Olympic Games back to the dream of [founder] Pierre de Coubertin, if indeed it is at all possible."[48]

Brundage would years later recall, "[At the Mexico City Olympics] warped mentalities and cracked personalities seemed to be everywhere, and impossible to eliminate." As the presidential election approached in the fall of 1968, the same could have been said of the American political sphere.[49]

five
Antiheroes

Despite political and logistical obstacles that had put him in a seemingly insurmountable hole only a few weeks earlier, Hubert Humphrey reached a virtual tie with Richard Nixon days before the election. His turnaround was attributable to party loyalty finally rising to the surface and to labor unions' ability to staunch the flow of blue-collar voters to the Wallace camp. But a major turning point came on September 30 in a Salt Lake City speech televised nationally by NBC. In his remarks, Humphrey finally carved out an independent position on Vietnam and expressed willingness to stop bombing in an effort to seek peace.

George Wallace's national polling numbers had climbed as high as 21 percent (they were much higher in the South), and he was still receiving daily piles of letters from devoted supporters. NBC News correspondent Douglas Kiker observed of Wallace's persistent popularity, "It is as if somewhere, sometime a while back, George Wallace had been awakened by a white blinding vision: they all hate black people, all of them. They're all afraid, all of them. Great God! That's it! They're all Southern! The whole United States

Third-party candidate presidential George Wallace *blew kisses to hecklers at an Oct. 8, 1968, campaign appearance in Baltimore, Md. (AP Photo)*

is Southern! Anybody who travels with Wallace these days on his presidential campaign finds it hard to resist arriving at the same conclusion."[1]

Wallace's support in Monroe, Michigan, an industrial town on Lake Erie, home to a Ford Motor Company components plant, stood at 27 percent. One man who worked at the plant said, "I'm not for him myself. You can't ship twenty million blacks out. You just can't kill them all. But up at Ford's, oh, I'd guess a third or more are for Wallace." While Wallace had dropped the overtly racist talk in favor of allusions to law and order and local control of schools, his message was still getting through. But Humphrey's late surge would coincide with Wallace's precipitous fall. The Independent candidate's collapse began

George Wallace, an avowed segregationist, appealed to millions of white, disaffected voters, carried five southern states, and won over 13% of the popular vote in the 1968 presidential election.

with his October 3 press conference in Pittsburgh, where he introduced his running mate, Gen. Curtis E. "Bombs Away" LeMay, the purported inspiration for Stanley Kubrick's psychotic character Gen. Buck Turgidson in the 1964 political satire *Dr. Strangelove.*[2]

LeMay told reporters at the press conference, "We must be willing to continue our bombing until we have destroyed every work of man in North Vietnam if that is what it takes to win the war." But his nonchalant discussion of deploying nuclear weapons raised eyebrows. "We seem to have a phobia about nuclear weapons," he said. "I don't believe the world would end if we exploded a nuclear weapon." Wallace tried to walk back LeMay's bellicose banter, insisting, "General LeMay hasn't advocated the use of nuclear weapons, not at all." But voters understood the general's words, and Wallace's popularity began a steady decline. Labor unions' efforts to remind members that Wallace's Alabama was hardly a workers' paradise only accelerated his downfall. Nearly ten million Americans would ultimately vote for Wallace, but the candidate would carry only the five Deep South states.[3]

President Johnson appeared to give Democrats a last-minute boost when he announced that bombing raids on North Vietnam would cease and that a new round of peace talks would begin the day after the election. But South Vietnamese officials deadened the impact of that news when they declared that their country would not participate in any peace negotiations. Rumors of shady dealings involving back-channel communication between Nixon's team and South Vietnam would be substantiated years later. Anna Chennault was a Chinese-born widow of the American commander of the Flying Tigers air unit in China during World War II. She was also a Nixon supporter and an active social hostess at her penthouse in the Watergate complex in Washington, DC. Chennault managed to leverage her connections to help convince her South Vietnamese contacts to sit out the talks and wait for the better deal that would come after Nixon's election.[4]

The bombing halt did help Humphrey, but not as much as it would have had South Vietnam been supportive. By the eve of the election, a Gallup poll had Humphrey trailing by just two points, and Harris gave him a slight edge. Ultimately, Nixon made the political calculation that he could win without significant support from the poor or from racial minorities. He was right, but just barely. Given Nixon's slim margin of victory, perhaps Chennault made a difference.

At 43.4 percent, Nixon was elected with the smallest share of the popular vote since Woodrow Wilson in 1912. The results remained in doubt through election night and into the following morning, but Humphrey finally conceded by telegram shortly after noon. Nixon's victory ushered in a decades-long conservative era in the American presidency in which a rhetorical skepticism of national government shaped the country's political discourse. But change was neither immediate nor complete.

It was the first time since Zachary Taylor's win in 1848 that a president had been elected without his party winning either house of Congress. But viewed from afar, the 1968 election is easily identified as an inflection point in the trajectory of American national politics. Nixon's victory ended a string of thirty-six years in which four Democrats and one moderate Republican had occupied the White House. In the sports realm, American football was experiencing a similar, if less universally significant, transformation in what was arguably the most important season in its history.

It might seem ironic that the most bellicose of American games, with its blitzes, bombs, trenches, and aerial attacks, was beginning to overtake baseball as the country's most popular team sport while the antiwar movement was gaining momentum. But the war protesters were merely a vocal minority, and the United States was hardly becoming a nation of pacifists. The most visible athlete in a new era of American professional football was the cocky New York Jets quarterback with a strange hint of a southern drawl. Joe Namath managed to bridge political and cultural divides in appealing to groups of people that might have agreed on little else. As James "Scotty" Reston, a Scottish-born,

***Richard Nixon**, pictured throwing a ceremonial first pitch at a Washington Senators game in 1969, won the 1968 presidential election with 43.4% of the popular vote. (Library of Congress)*

American-educated political reporter and newspaper executive, explained, Namath "defies both the people who hate playboys and the people who hate bullyboys. He is something special: a long-haired hard-hat, the anti-hero of the sports world."[5]

Namath was sufficiently audacious and antiauthoritarian to make headlines on and off the field, even in the crowded news environment of 1968. Though critics often contemptuously labeled him a hippie, Namath avoided taking public stances on partisan matters. Whether attributable more to his political restraint or to his skin color, Namath also managed to escape the ripe disdain many fans felt for Muhammad Ali, Tommie Smith, or John Carlos. Namath had plenty of detractors, but he became commercially marketable in a way that other controversial stars of the era could not.

Joe Namath grew up in Beaver Falls, Pennsylvania, a steel town thirty-five miles northwest of Pittsburgh. His father had emigrated from Hungary as a child, worked in a local steel mill, and left Joe's mother when Joe, the youngest of four brothers and an adopted sister, was in seventh grade. The young Namath excelled at baseball, basketball, and football. But he also made a name for himself as something of a town rogue, wiling much of his time away in the local pool hall. He quit the high school basketball team his senior year after his old-school coach removed him from a game for showboating—driving to the basket, flamboyantly dunking the ball, and theatrically tossing it to the referee. Rather than taking a seat on the bench at the coach's behest, Namath strode straight to the locker room, never to return. As biographer Mark Kriegel wrote, "No one had seen anything like that before—not in the mills or the churches or the schools, and certainly not on the fields or in the gyms. A coach's authority was almost absolute, less frequently challenged than a boss's or a priest's or a cop's." The team lost the remainder of its games that season.[6]

Namath received offers from several clubs to play professional baseball out of high school, but he elected to pursue football and attend college, in part to please his mother. Nearly all the powerhouse programs recruited him, and Namath decided on the University of Maryland. But his plans changed after he failed to meet the school's SAT requirements. When word reached the University of Alabama that Namath might be available, legendary Crimson Tide head coach Bear Bryant sent his assistant Howard Schnellenberger to Pennsylvania to lure the star quarterback to Tuscaloosa. It took him longer than he expected, but after a few days in Beaver Falls, Schnellenberger got Namath on a southbound plane.

On his first trip to campus in 1961, Namath watched a session of summer practice. He wore a tight brown checked suit with a pocket watch, carried a pack of Kools in his breast pocket, and sported a feather-adorned blue fedora on his head. Peering through sunglasses, a toothpick dangling from his mouth, he climbed the stairs to the tower where Bear Bryant observed practice from on high. No one could remember anyone joining Bryant in his crow's nest, let alone a walking spectacle like this freshman-to-be.

Paul Bryant had grown up in Moro Bottom, Arkansas, and earned his nickname by wrestling a bear at a local carnival as a teenager. He also won everywhere he coached. At the University of Kentucky, he supposedly responded to a player complaining about a broken hand by shouting, "You don't run on your hands, do you?" Bryant cemented his demanding reputation in his first year as Texas A&M head coach. One hundred fifteen players began his preseason training camp in Junction, Texas, that year. Only thirty-five remained at the start of the season. The team then lost nine of its ten games but gained lasting fame as the "Junction Boys." Bryant left A&M when he was offered the head job at his alma mater, Alabama. The Bear was set to begin his fourth season in Tuscaloosa when Namath came for his campus visit. The pair had a long conversation, little of which Namath could understand due to the coach's thick southern drawl. But what he heard was good enough to convince Namath that Alabama was the place for him, and he initiated the enrollment process that day.[7]

Bryant took to calling Namath "Joe Willie," an improvement on the first nickname that had attached to him. Many of the athlete's teammates called him "Nigger"—a reference to some combination of his olive skin and the photo in his dorm room of a young woman of color from his hometown. Joe Willie had a good ring to it, and it made the Pennsylvanian seem like less of an outsider and more of a good ole boy. Segregated public accommodations in Alabama were unfamiliar to Namath, who had been the only white starter on his high school basketball team. However, he soon adapted to the new environment and thrived socially and athletically.

Namath compiled a 29–4 record as a starter at Alabama, including a win in the Orange Bowl as a sophomore. That summer, Namath was on campus when President Kennedy federalized the Alabama National Guard and ordered the troops to remove Gov. George Wallace from the doorway of Foster Auditorium, where he was preventing the school's first black undergraduate students from registering for summer classes. When Namath was suspended late the following season for breaking unspecified team rules, rumors swirled that he was being punished for dating Vivian Malone, the female student of color at Alabama. But the pair barely knew each other and certainly were not dating. The suspension concerned an alcohol-related infraction, which caused

Namath to miss his team's win over the University of Mississippi in the Sugar Bowl. But he returned for his senior year and set school passing records for attempts, completions, yardage, and touchdowns in a career.

That year Alabama was voted national champion without having played a game against a team with a black player. While this schedule was not unusual in the all-white Southeastern Conference, some writers believed it tarnished Bama's achievement. Jim Murray wrote, "So Alabama is the National Champion, is it? Hah! 'National' champion of what? The Confederacy? This team hasn't poked its head above the Mason-Dixon line since Appomattox. This team wins the Front-of-the-Bus championship every year."[8]

In drafts held simultaneously on November 28, 1964, Namath was taken twelfth by the NFL's St. Louis Cardinals but picked first by the New York Jets of the rival American Football League. The Jets had been called the New York Titans the year before but had filed for bankruptcy and had then been acquired by a new ownership group. The team's new name signaled a new start for the flagging franchise. The AFL had been founded in 1959 by a group of wealthy businessmen who had been shut out of the NFL ownership fraternity. The eight-team upstart league struggled in its first few years but was relatively flush after inking a $36 million contract with NBC. Armed with television cash, AFL owners looked to prevent the NFL from signing top college players, with the ultimate objective of forcing a merger with the older league.

Coach Bryant told Namath to ask for a $200,000 contract. "Hell, you may not get it, but it's a good place to start," he told his quarterback. Representatives from the Cardinals showed up at Namath's dorm room to discuss his signing. Namath mumbled something about $200,000 and a car, and they quickly departed, feigning indignant disbelief. A few days later they contacted Namath and sounded amenable to his terms if he would sign immediately, before talking to the Jets. Bryant advised against rashness. Namath decided to hire as an agent his lawyer friend, a former student manager for the Alabama football team named Mike Bite, who soon began negotiations with the Jets.[9]

The managing partner of the new Jets' ownership group, Sonny Werblin, was enthusiastically crafting a new image for the New York club. He changed the franchise name and moved the team from the decrepit Polo Grounds in Harlem to Shea Stadium, the Mets' new ballpark in Queens, near La Guardia Airport. Werblin had made his fortune in the entertainment industry as an executive at the Music Corporation of America (MCA) and later became one of the most powerful people in the television industry.

Werblin recognized star power when he saw it, and he saw it in Namath. "In all my theatrical experience," he said, "I've met few Hollywood stars with the indefinable quality of being able to walk into a room and electrify everyone there by the magnetism of their presence—Clark Gable, Gregory Peck, Joan Crawford and Marilyn Monroe. It's the same quality that Jack Dempsey and Babe Ruth had. My feeling is that Namath has much of the demeanor and attitude of Joe DiMaggio."[10]

If Werblin could sign Namath, one of the most talented passers in recent memory, it would be a victory for the AFL, helping to raise the visibility of the league that hoped to showcase its pass-happy style as an attractive alternative to the stodgier NFL. Werblin flew Namath and his agent to California to watch the Jets play the Chargers. The actor who played the Lone Ranger on television, Clayton Moore, drove the young men to the game. Later that evening, Academy Award–winning actress Jane Wyman, the ex-wife of Ronald Reagan, joined Namath, Bite, and Werblin at dinner. Bite told Werblin that he wanted a half million for Namath, and they eventually settled on a figure just north of $400,000, including a Jet-green Lincoln Continental convertible and jobs for three of Namath's family members. It was the most lucrative contract in the history of American team sports, but Werblin was happy to pay, as the deal had come with priceless publicity for his franchise. "It's something I learned from my theatrical experiences," Werblin said. "You can't do things cheaply. A million-dollar set is worthless if you put a $2,000 actor in the main role."[11]

Namath's record-setting contract put the NFL on notice that the AFL would stop at nothing to attract top collegiate players, and it accelerated the leagues' march toward merger that would be announced the following year. But the contract would remain unpublicized and unsigned until after Alabama's New Year's Day 1965 appearance in the Orange Bowl—the first bowl game to be broadcast in prime time and "in living color"—so that Namath would maintain his eligibility to participate as an amateur.

A sellout crowd filled the Miami stadium, and a record-setting television audience tuned in to see Alabama and the Texas Longhorns. George Wallace and Richard Nixon sat in the stands, and comedian Jackie Gleason handled the coin toss. Namath began the game on the bench, having reinjured his knee in practice that week. Earlier in the season he had torn a meniscus and strained a ligament in the knee that would give him serious trouble the rest of his career. "Joe moves like a human now," Bryant told the press after the injury. "He moved like a cat before."[12]

When Texas jumped out to a 14–0 lead, Bryant summoned Namath from the bench. Despite a cumbersome knee brace that limited his mobility, Namath guided the Tide on an eighty-seven-yard scoring drive. Alabama scored on its first possession of the second half, cutting a 21–7 Texas halftime lead to 21–14 and prompting Werblin to note of Namath, "Fabulous, fabulous, fabulous. Reminds me of [Baltimore Colts quarterback Johnny] Unitas." Midway through the fourth quarter, with Texas ahead 21–17, Alabama intercepted a tipped pass at the Texas thirty-four yard line. Namath led the Tide to the shadows of the Texas goal line before the Longhorns stopped him a foot from a score on a fourth-down sneak that would have given Alabama a late lead.[13]

Despite not throwing a touchdown, being intercepted twice, and not playing for the winning team, Namath was named the game's most valuable player. "The 72,647 who filled the Orange Bowl Stadium were privileged to witness an exhibition that has hardly been surpassed in artistry, unruffled poise and deadly targetry," the *New York Times* raved. University of Texas coach Darryl K. Royal called Namath's play "the most courageous by any player [he'd] ever seen."[14]

Later that week the Jets held an event introducing the New York media to Namath at Toots Shor's, a Manhattan night spot popular with aging athletes and the writers who covered them. The press wanted Namath to talk about his contract, but he deflected questions that pried too specifically. One writer asked whether Namath would still be able to keep all the money if he failed to "make it" as a professional football player. "I'll make it," Namath replied. His self-confidence often spilled into the realm of arrogance, and he was simply uninterested in playing the older generation's game of false modesty with the press. By the standard of revolutionary loquaciousness Muhammad Ali had set, Namath was a mere amateur. But even Namath's level of brashness was groundbreaking in the conservative world of American professional team sports.[15]

Not everyone considered Namath's contract to be money well spent for the Jets, but everyone had an opinion. In the *New York Times*, Arthur Daley called the deal "utterly ridiculous." "No untried collegian is worth half that much," he declared. But Olympic gold medalist sprinter Bob Hayes, who had starred as a wide receiver at Florida A&M and played with Namath in the Senior Bowl, said the quarterback was "worth every penny" and called him "[the] best passer I have ever seen." The *New York Daily News*'s Dick Young concurred with the assessment: "After a look at Joe Namath in pulsating color, I'm convinced of one thing. The Jets aren't paying him enough. He's a steal at $400,000, and if Sonny Werblin were decent about it, he'd toss in a membership card to the Playboy Club because Joe is said to have a wholesome interest in bunnies."[16]

Later that winter Namath underwent knee surgery to remove cartilage and tighten a ligament. The doctor declared the procedure a success but told the team that Namath had the knees of a seventy-year-old. That summer the quarterback appeared on the cover of *Sports Illustrated* beneath the headline

Joe Namath trotting to the locker room following the New York Jets 16–7 win over the heavily favored Baltimore Colts in Super Bowl III on Jan. 12, 1969. Namath famously guaranteed that the Jets would win, and his fulfillment of that promise vaulted him into a celebrity status that transcended sports. Unlike many top athletes that year, Namath managed to stay above the political fray. (AP Photo/NFL Photo)

"Football Goes Showbiz." The image depicted Namath in his Jets uniform at the intersection of Broadway and Seventh Avenue with the bright lights of Times Square in the background. In the article, writer Robert Boyle described Namath as "a real ring-ding-a-ding finger snapper, a girl ogler, a swingin' cat with dark good looks who sleeps till noon" and whose "major interests are 'girls and golf, girls and golf.'"[17]

The rookie's excessive early exposure, combined with his hefty salary, gave veteran teammates plenty of ammunition with which to harass him. In that environment, the name "Broadway Joe" quickly attached to Namath. He hardly shied away from special treatment. In an era when crew cuts were nearly universal on the football field, Namath kept his hair long. At a time when football players uniformly wore black shoes, Namath had wrapped his in medical tape at Alabama. As a pro, he no longer had to use tape; the Jets' equipment manager arranged for special white shoes to be made for Broadway Joe.

A bar-owning, season ticket–holding friend of Namath's named Barry Skolnick recalled that many fans initially hesitated to embrace the flashy quarterback. "Everybody was yelling that Joe was a fag because he wore white shoes," Skolnick said. "The fans were pretty rough on him." Despite the criticism, Namath was in no hurry to capitulate to anyone's expectations, particularly not as to the color of his footwear. "For me to change at that point would be punking out, man," Namath said. "I don't punk out."[18]

A feature piece the following year in *Sports Illustrated* helped to introduce American sports fans to Namath's off-field persona:

Stoop-Shouldered and sinisterly handsome, he slouches against the wall of the saloon, a filter cigarette in his teeth, collar open, perfectly happy and self-assured, gazing through the uneven darkness to sort out the winners from the losers. As the girls come by wearing their miniskirts, net stockings, big false eyelashes, long pressed hair and soulless expressions, he grins approvingly and says, 'Hey, hold it, man—foxes.' It is Joe Willie Namath at play. Relaxing. Night-timing. The boss mover studying the defensive tendencies of New York's off-duty secretaries, stewardesses, dancers, nurses, Playboy bunnies, actresses, shopgirls—all of the people who make life stimulating for a bachelor who can throw one of the best passes in pro football. He poses a question for us all: Would you rather be young, single, rich, famous, talented and happy—or president?"[19]

In a different era, Namath would have been hailed as a hardworking kid from a blue-collar background who played by the rules to achieve a slice of the American Dream. But he did not neatly fit that mold. He was not humble. He did not hide his enjoyment of alcohol and women. But neither did Namath play the role of antiestablishment reprobate. When a reporter asked him whether he was a rebel, the quarterback demurred. "If I don't believe in something, though, I'm not gonna go along with it," he said. "It has nothing to do with being anti-establishment or whatever; it's just that if it's not right for me, then I can't go along with it. I'm not trying to fight society—I'm just trying to be myself."

It would have been exceedingly difficult for any athlete in the mid- to late 1960s to become the transcendent celebrity, product endorser, and star of television and film that Namath became if that athlete had been perceived as either unusually conservative or radically liberal. Many people found Namath's swagger off-putting, and plenty in the older generation deemed his hair length an indication of at least a vaguely antiauthoritarian bent. But no one could categorically label him either an antiwar zealot or an archconservative. Namath was captivating without posing any fundamental threat to the American social structure. He was the right person at the right time to bring professional football into the national spotlight.

For all the attention and accolades that he would later receive, Namath's on-field tenure with the Jets began without distinction. He did not play in the season opener in Houston despite starter Mike Taliaferro's completing only four of twenty-one passes. Namath had some catching up to do, but he would prove to be a quick study. He threw his first professional touchdown pass in week two of his rookie year and soon established himself as the most promising young passer in the league. But as the United States continued to increase its military commitment to South Vietnam, even a budding football superstar was not immune to the draft.

Upon leaving Alabama, Namath's draft status had been reclassified to 1-A, and he was required to report to the Armed Services Induction Center in lower Manhattan early in his rookie season. If he passed the exam, his induction would be imminent. President Johnson had recently called for more bodies in Vietnam, and Namath was neither married nor a student. A reporter with the New York Journal-American asked Namath whether he would consider marriage to avoid the draft. "I don't even have a steady girlfriend," a smiling Namath replied. "I'd rather fight those reds in Vietnam than get married. Too many pretty girls in this world."[20]

After four hours of physical examinations, followed by more evaluation three weeks later, the doctors unanimously determined that Namath's knee rendered him unfit for military service. When word reached the public, many were outraged. The army issued an explanation, hoping to fend off any suspicion of favorable treatment for a budding football star: "It may seem illogical that an individual who is physically active in civilian athletics should be found unfit for military service," the statement read. "When playing professional football, it must be presumed that Mr. Namath does so with the counsel and preparation of doctors and trainers. He is closely watched and professional assistance is close at hand at every game and practice session. In the military service, these conditions would not necessarily be present. In Vietnam, for example, the life and safety of his comrades could depend on Namath performing his duties under extremely adverse conditions."[21]

The army's justification did not satisfy everyone. On the House floor, a Florida congressman verbalized his objections to what he saw as special treatment. He entered into the congressional record a letter from a constituent whose son was serving on the front lines in Vietnam despite being plagued by a high school football injury. "I would like to know," the correspondent stated, "why there is no menial duty that can be given to physical weaklings such as Joe Namath . . . so the physical giants such as my son can be freed to fight our country's battles." He concluded by calling Namath's reclassification "the most asinine action of the year."[22]

The House Armed Services Committee quickly launched an investigation into procedures to determine draft statuses of famous athletes, and soon thereafter Muhammad Ali's status was reclassified to 1-A. Namath refused to let criticism cow him. "How can I win, man?" he asked *Sports Illustrated*'s Dan Jenkins. "If I say I'm glad, I'm a traitor, and if I say I'm sorry, I'm a fool." Mickey Mantle had been classified as unfit to serve in the Korean War due to osteomyelitis (a rare bone infection) in his left ankle that he had been diagnosed with in high school. After standards were altered such that someone with a past history of that ailment could serve, Mantle was again found unfit for military service. His second exemption owed to the knee injury he had suffered in the 1951 World Series. The Yankee slugger did receive some public criticism over his classification, but it lacked the venom Namath's draft status generated.[23]

Namath began his first season coming off the bench but led the team to a 5–3 finish as a starter and was named the AFL's rookie of the year. No less an authority than Vince Lombardi touted Namath's talent. "His arm, his release of the ball are just perfect," Lombardi said. "Namath is as good a passer as I've ever seen." During AFL broadcasts, which included innovative use of on-field cameras, television producers followed Namath even after plays were finished. Fans watching on television could catch Joe on the sidelines, helmet removed, as he chewed gum, warmed up, or talked on the phone to a coach in the press box. "We isolated the cameras on him all the time," an NBC executive explained. "Everything we could do, however we could do it, instant replay, whatever. He was the guy we were going to highlight. The lead story was going to be Joe."[24]

Namath quickly justified the lavish expense of his contract in season-ticket sales alone, not to mention the increased visibility for the league. The summer before his second season, the AFL and NFL announced a merger that would include a championship game at the end of the season and full integration beginning in 1970. Oakland Raiders owner Al Davis, a former AFL commissioner, said simply, "Namath made us." Arthur Daley, who was generally no fan of Namath, once calling him a "spoiled brat," agreed. Daley wrote of Werblin's decision to sign Namath, "With one gesture, he saved the Jets, saved the AFL, and set the wheels spinning inexorably along the road to merger."[25]

Namath led the league in passing the next two years. He also became the first professional quarterback to throw for four thousand yards in a season, despite dealing with near-constant pain from two bad knees that he tried to manage with cortisone, Butazolidin, and scotch. His name and face had become recognizable even to non–football fans. Unlike star athletes of previous generations, Namath felt no need to hide his carousing from the press. Reporters were only too happy to cover any aspect of his life, from his hair and beard length to the comings and goings at the bachelor pad he shared with turf writer Joe Hirsch and former Alabama teammate Ray Abruzzese. The Upper East Side apartment was professionally decorated with a leather bar, llama rug, snow leopard pillows, suede couches, and an oval-shaped bed. Guests came and went at all hours for varied entertainment that could include a dice game or a boozy soiree on any given night.

"Some people don't like this image I got myself, bein' a swinger," Namath said. "They see me with a girl instead of being home like other athletes. But I'm not institutional. I swing. It hasn't hurt my friends or my family and it hasn't hurt me. So why hide it? It's the truth." In the course of his swinging, Namath managed to catch the attention of the FBI when an agent saw him playing liar's poker with known mobsters at a popular New York night spot. Namath would later land on a White House list of people "not in sympathy with the policies and goals of the Nixon Administration." The infamous list would eventually include hundreds of names, and he was the only athlete on it. FBI director J. Edgar Hoover once said, "You won't find long hair or sideburns a la Joe Namath here. There are no hippies [in the FBI]." [26]

Namath's record-setting passing prowess in 1967 powered the Jets to an 8–5–1 record. Though they fell one win short of the playoffs, the future looked promising. But before the start of the 1968 season, infighting among the team's owners led to Sonny Werblin's selling his interest in the Jets. The new group offered Vince Lombardi the opportunity to be coach, general manager, or both. Fresh off his consecutive Super Bowl victories with the Packers, Lombardi turned down the offer. With Werblin gone, Namath was even less constrained in his pursuit of fun and attention that irritated some of his teammates. He secured an endorsement deal with a furrier to wear a $5,000 mink coat, which he modeled at training camp that summer. Namath and two unmarried friends also opened a cocktail lounge on Lexington Avenue near Sixty-Second Street called Bachelors III.

New York Times football writer William Wallace called for Namath to be traded before the start of the season, citing the quarterback's "wobbly knees," and his "alienated relationship" with head coach Weeb Eubank in the wake of Sonny Werblin's departure. The Jets did not heed the writer's advice, and Namath assumed new leadership responsibilities on the team. After never finishing higher than fourth in player voting for the team MVP award, the quarterback was elected team captain for the 1968 season.[27]

Though some speculated that the new ownership group may have encouraged the players to select Namath, the gesture nevertheless moved him; he called it the greatest honor of his life. Despite his extracurricular antics, Namath was one of the few Jets who could unite various factions of the team, and he traveled freely among linemen and backs, blacks and whites, northerners and southerners. "He really got along with the black guys," recalled former *New York Post* football writer Paul Zimmerman. "He'd come off the cafeteria line with his tray and go straight for the black table, integrating it. I saw him do that so many times I know it wasn't an accident. He was way ahead of his time."[28]

The 1968 season began somewhat inauspiciously for Namath, as he missed on six of his first seven pass attempts in the Jets' opener in Kansas City. Even so, New York held on to beat the talented Chiefs by a point. The following week the team trounced the lowly Patriots 47–31, but Namath completed only thirteen passes. Jets defensive back Jim Hudson told Namath that he was going to try abstaining from alcohol for the rest of the season and encouraged Namath to join him. The quarterback agreed to a trial run for the remainder of the week, which he found inconvenient given the amount of time he had become accustomed to spending at his new bar. The next game, Buffalo beat the Jets for their lone win of the season. Namath completed only nineteen of forty-three passes and threw five interceptions, three of which the Bills returned for touchdowns.

Thus ended Namath's four-and-a-half-day experiment with sobriety. "I started drinking again that night, and I drank right through the following Sunday when I threw no interceptions and we whipped San Diego," he said. When he threw five interceptions at Denver the following week, on the heels of a bout with the flu that had kept him out of the bar for a few days, Namath was further convinced of the inadvisability of alcohol abstinence. But in solidarity with teammates who had pledged to avoid shaving until New York clinched the division title, Joe grew a Fu Manchu. The Jets won their next four games to run their record to 7–2. They then traveled to face the top team in the West, the Oakland Raiders. The game would produce one of the most memorable endings in football history, though most fans were unable to see it.[29]

The evenly matched teams went back and forth for most of the afternoon before the Jets kicked a field goal with a little over a minute remaining to take a 32–29 lead. The Raiders connected on a quick twenty-one-yard pass with a face mask penalty tacked onto the end, and Oakland found itself on the Jets' forty-three with fifty seconds on the clock. At 7 p.m. on the east coast, with the outcome in the balance, NBC abandoned its broadcast of the game in order to air *Heidi*, sponsored by Timex watches and starring Jennifer Edwards as an orphan girl living with her grandfather in the Swiss Alps. "You treated a sponsor like that very carefully because you wanted them to come back," said NBC's supervisor on duty. "And since it was 'only' AFL football and nobody was really sure how many viewers watched it anyway, it seemed like the thing to do." The livid fans, who "literally blew out the network switchboard" with their angry phone calls, disagreed.[30]

Unbeknownst to the millions who had been watching on television, the Raiders scored a touchdown to take the lead, then returned a fumble on the ensuing kickoff for another touchdown—all in nine seconds. Thus Oakland not only won the game but also covered the seven-and-a-half-point spread. The fallout from the Heidi game led to NBC's promise to show all games to their conclusion and demonstrated the popularity of the AFL and of professional football in America.

The week after the Heidi game the AFL league office pressured Namath to "conform with the generally accepted idea of an American athlete's appearance" with regard to his unusual moustache. But the facial hair stayed, and the Jets beat the Chargers 37–15 to clinch at least a tie in the AFL's Eastern Division. Namath finally shaved on December 11, after an appearance on the *Tonight Show*. His price for shaving on camera, paid by Schick razors for use in an ad campaign, was $10,000.[31]

The Jets ended the 1968 regular season with four straight wins to finish at 11–3, and Namath was named league MVP. New York avenged its Heidi game loss to the Raiders in the AFL Championship game to advance to the Super Bowl. There the Jets would face the formidable Baltimore Colts, champions of the NFL. Early betting lines favored the Colts by seventeen points, and by game day some bettors were getting as many as twenty. Many pundits were calling the Colt defense the best in the history of the sport, and few gave the Jets any real chance at victory. Baltimore had lost only once all season and had shut out the Cleveland Browns 34–0 to take the NFL championship. Gamblers who wanted to bet on a Jets win were getting 7-1 odds. No line on a major American sporting event had been that lopsided since Cassius Clay fought

Sonny Liston in 1964. Howard Cosell predicted a 30–10 victory for the Colts, while other prognosticators doubted the Jets would even score.

"I didn't know we were that bad a football team," Namath said when asked about the point spread. "I might sound like I'm boasting and bragging, and I am. Ask anybody who's played against us in our league. The Colts are good, but we're good."[32]

The Jets checked into the Galt Ocean Mile resort in Fort Lauderdale ten days before Super Bowl III would be played at the Orange Bowl in Miami. Namath and his roommate Jim Hudson took the Governor's Suite, where Vince Lombardi had stayed for the previous year's big game. "I'm not sure he would have approved of everything I did in his old room," Namath later said. The team used the New York Yankees' spring training facility for workouts, and Namath was assigned Mickey Mantle's locker. Though he managed to enjoy his stay, the quarterback must have been at least mildly unnerved when FBI agents came to his room to inform him of threats on his life, possibly involving the Miami criminal underground.[33]

The first night in Florida, Namath nearly came to blows with Colts kicker Lou Michaels after they argued in a bar about Catholicism, each other's mothers, and who would win the game the following Sunday. "We're gonna kick the shit out of you, and I'm gonna do it," Joe said. Michaels suggested they take their discussion to the parking lot, but teammates intervened. Joe ended up buying the drinks and giving Michaels a ride back to his hotel. The next morning, Namath could not be roused for a team photo session. "If they want pictures of me," he told his roommate, "they're going to have to take 'em later than ten o'clock." As he subsequently explained to the press, "I always sleep in the morning, that's the thing to do. You've got to get your rest." Namath held court by the hotel pool, where he entertained journalists all week. His confident banter notwithstanding, forty-nine of fifty-five writers picked the Colts to win the game.[34]

Some of the Colts seemed to feel the burden of heavy favoritism. Coach Don Shula told reporters, "Everything we accomplished this season goes on the line at 3 o'clock on Sunday. If we blow it, everything is destroyed." The perception of NFL superiority was widespread, and the Colts needed to win big to uphold the standard Lombardi's Packers had set in the first two Super Bowls.[35]

Namath received treatment on both knees all week, including injections of prednisone, a regimen to which he was all too accustomed. Thursday night Namath accepted the Miami Touchdown Club's Player of the Year Award in the King Arthur Banquet Room at the Miami Springs Villas. Before taking the stage to offer some remarks, he had imbibed a few glasses of scotch during cocktail hour and some beer at a team barbecue that afternoon. After Namath thanked "all the single girls in New York for their contribution," a heckler yelled at the quarterback to sit down. "Who's that," Namath asked, "Lou Michaels?" Then he added, "The Jets will win Sunday, I guarantee it."[36]

Namath's famous guarantee made the *Miami Herald* the next morning. Newspapers across the country also published his remarks in weekend previews, giving the game a compelling context and story line, which NBC play-by-play man Curt Gowdy referenced in his broadcast introduction. Despite expert consensus on the likelihood of a runaway win by the Colts, bookies did brisk business.

Outside the ranks of Colts and Jets fans, rooting interest in the game tended to be tied to one's general opinion of Namath. Some saw a flippant show-off without reverence for sacred traditions of American sport. Others saw a refreshing departure from the hypocrisy of an older generation of star athletes. Devotees of short-cropped hair and all that it symbolized tended to gravitate toward the Colts. Many younger and hipper fans cheered for the Jets.

The vice president–elect, Spiro Agnew, was among the sellout crowd of over seventy-five thousand at the Orange Bowl, as a guest of Bob Hope. Predictably, Agnew backed the Colts; he was the former governor of Maryland. Joseph P. Kennedy sat in the stands with his lone surviving son, Teddy, who was a friend of Colts owner Carroll Rosenbloom. Advertisers, including Chrysler, Pall Mall, Salem, Winston, TWA, RCA, Phillips 66, Schlitz, and Gillette, paid more than $100,000 per minute to sell products to the forty million Americans watching the televised spectacle at home.

On the Colts' first possession, Lou Michaels missed a short field goal, an early indication that the week-long wars of words and media clatter had affected some of Baltimore's players more than they had let on. After a scoreless first quarter, the Colts had the ball deep in Jets territory. But an interception on a tipped pass ended the scoring threat. New York then drove eighty yards for a touchdown, taking advantage of a Colts blitzing scheme that Namath had identified as exploitable in film sessions that week. Baltimore responded with another sustained drive and another missed field goal by Michaels. The Colts' next possession ended in another interception, this one at the Jets two yard line, and New York took a 7–0 lead into the halftime locker room.

The Colts fumbled in their first play from scrimmage in the second half, and the Jets held the ball for all but three minutes of the third quarter, adding two field goals to stretch their lead to 13–0. At that point, Colts coach Don Shula summoned Johnny Unitas from the bench. The three-time NFL MVP had made a name for himself in an overtime victory against the New York Giants in the 1958 NFL championship game, and he was the greatest quarterback of the late '50s and early '60s. Unitas had been Namath's boyhood hero and remained one of the sport's all-time greats, but he had missed most of the season with an arm injury. The thirty-five-year-old was probably past his prime even when healthy, and his first series of the day lasted only three plays. With Namath nursing an injured thumb, the Jets did not run a pass play the entire fourth quarter. They took a 16–0 lead on Jim Turner's third field goal of the afternoon, and after Unitas threw an interception in the end zone, Gowdy told his NBC audience that they could be witnessing one of the greatest upsets in sports history.

Unitas led Baltimore on an eighty-yard touchdown drive to make the score 16–7 with three minutes and nineteen seconds to play, but the late attempt at a comeback would fall short. After recovering Lou Michaels's onside kick, the Colts could advance no farther than the Jets' nineteen before turning the ball over on downs. As he jogged to the locker room after postgame congratulations, Namath shook his extended index finger at the crowd, confirming that he and the Jets were number one.

The headline in the *Miami Herald* sports section the next morning read "JOE GUARANTEED IT." Sportswriter Larry Merchant later summed up the impact of Namath's accomplishment: "For three hours 75 million [*sic*] viewers on television saw the end of the world as they knew it. And it blew their minds. They had been convinced by the pro football mystique that a quarterback had to be Bart Starr or Johnny Unitas to win championships, leading by example, modesty, discipline, character and attendance at communion breakfasts. . . . For the fans who bought that theology whole, it was a three-hour horror show. . . . Namath changed the face of professional football with one orgasmic victory."[37]

Howard Cosell acknowledged his wayward prediction for the game and explained the upset in terms of David and Goliath. "What I really saw," he told the *ABC Evening News* audience, "was the end of an era, the death of the establishment."[38] Outside the realm of professional football, the establishment was doing just fine. Richard Nixon was inaugurated eight days later as the thirty-seventh president of the United States.

Epilogue

The Jets' Super Bowl victory vaulted Joe Namath into a celebrity status typically reserved for Hollywood stars or pop music icons. He became the most marketable athlete in America and among the most recognized figures in the nation. Fans flooded hotel lobbies, airport terminals, and anywhere Namath was scheduled to appear. In addition to his Manhattan bar, he soon had an ownership stake in a chain of hamburger restaurants called Broadway Joe's, a weekly television show, a clothing line, film roles, and a book deal. Along with Mickey Mantle, Namath even lent his name to the employment agency Mantle Men and Namath Girls. The business would become the second-biggest temp service in the world.

That summer Namath would briefly retire from football. After it had become clear that the regular clientele at Bachelors III included prostitutes, fraudsters, and—most troubling to the NFL—gamblers, the league told him to either sell his interest in the bar or face a suspension. Various law enforcement agencies had surveilled Namath's establishment, and NFL commissioner Pete Rozelle felt that the quarterback's association with Bachelors III damaged the league's image. Namath's retirement made the news summary that White House aides placed on President Nixon's desk each morning. Nixon liked to annotate the pages of the briefings, and he wrote, "Good riddance. These guys must set an example" next to the Namath story.[1]

Namath and the league eventually reached a compromise that allowed him to return to the Jets for the start of the season. Still, knee problems would bother him for the rest of his career. Though he would still be reasonably productive as a quarterback when Nixon resigned from the presidency amid scandal in 1974, Namath never again reached the heights that he had in the Jets' championship season. But the new version of American sports celebrity that Namath helped craft would remain attached to him long after his football days were finished. In the late sixties, such a transcendent athlete almost had to be white. But black superstar athletes including O.J. Simpson, Michael Jordan, and Tiger Woods would later follow in Namath's footsteps as business friendly endorsement machines who chose to conspicuously avoid partisan politics.

When Vince Lombardi retired from coaching the Packers following Green Bay's win in Super Bowl II, he was worn down from various ailments, including digestive problems, heartburn, degenerative arthritis in his hip, and an ulcer related to long-term use of pain medication. He also complained of chest pains and shortness of breath. Lombardi was fifty-four years old but looked two decades older. He would return to the sidelines in 1969 and lead the Washington Redskins to their first winning season in over a decade. But the following summer he was diagnosed with terminal cancer. Less than three years after the Packers' Ice Bowl triumph, Lombardi was on his deathbed, where he was heard feverishly muttering, "Joe Namath! You're not bigger than football! Remember that!"[2]

The Jets' Super Bowl win had helped ensure that the AFL-NFL merger would be deemed competitively legitimate when it was fully consummated in 1970. It also kept professional football on a trajectory that would allow it to move ahead of baseball as the most popular and culturally significant American spectator sport. In its October 14, 1968 issue, *Newsweek* featured an article entitled "The Great National Bore" in which sportswriter Pete Axthelm noted, "Baseball's problem is that it is the national pastime, while football and basketball can lay more legitimate claims to be national *sports*. And in America in 1968, how many people are still seeking slow-paced, relatively undemanding ways to merely pass the time?"[3]

Beginning the following season, Major League Baseball owners collectively decided to lower the mound and tighten the strike zone in an attempt to swing the balance of power from pitchers toward hitters. They hoped this change would produce more offense and serve as a remedy for falling attendance figures. The American and National Leagues were also split in two divisions whose winners would play at the end of the season for a chance to compete in the World Series. Thus the 1968 Series was the last in which the regular-season champions of each league would square off without an intermediary round of playoffs. New major-league teams in Kansas City, Seattle, Montreal, and San Diego would also begin play in 1969, further expanding MLB's presence beyond its traditional base in the East and Midwest.

Following the 1969 season, the St. Louis Cardinals traded all-star outfielder Curt Flood to the Philadelphia Phillies. Flood was happy in St. Louis and did not want to play in Philadelphia, which had gained a reputation as being unwelcoming to black ballplayers. Flood decided that he would take a stand and contest the trade, seeking redress in court if necessary. At a Players Association executive board meeting, Flood was asked whether he was challenging his trade for the betterment of the players or as a broader political statement. "I think the change in black consciousness in recent years has made me more sensitive to the injustice in every area of my life," Flood replied. "But I want you to know that what I'm doing here I'm doing as a ball player, and I think

St. Louis Cardinal outfielder *Curt Flood's lawsuit against Major League Baseball helped to hasten the arrival of free agency in the sport, which would eventually allow players to negotiate for higher pay and better working conditions. (AP Photo)*

it's absolutely terrible that we have stood by and watched this situation go on for so many years and never pulled together to do anything about it."[4]

As Flood explained in Ken Burns's 1994 documentary *Baseball*, "I guess you really have to understand who that person, who that Curt Flood was. I'm a child of the Sixties, a man of the Sixties. During that period of time, this country was coming apart at the seams. We were in Southeast Asia. Men, good men, were dying for America and for the Constitution. In the Southern part of the United States, we were marching for civil rights, and Dr. King had been assassinated, and we lost the Kennedys. And to think that merely because I was a professional baseball player I could ignore what was going on outside the walls of Busch Stadium is truly hypocrisy. And now I find that all of those rights that these great Americans were dying for, I didn't have in my own profession."[5]

On Christmas Eve Flood sent a letter to baseball commissioner Bowie Kuhn, who earlier in the year had replaced the embattled Spike Eckert. "After twelve years in the major leagues, I do not feel that I am a piece of property to be bought and sold irrespective of my wishes," Flood wrote. "I believe that any system which produces that result violates my basic rights as a citizen and is inconsistent with the laws of the United States and of the several states."[6]

Kuhn was not sympathetic to Flood's grievance. A 1922 Supreme Court decision had dubiously held that baseball was not subject to federal antitrust laws because it was a sport rather than a business and because any interstate commerce involved was "incidental" to the games. In light of that precedent, the commissioner had every reason to believe that US courts would continue to enforce the reserve clause in players' contracts, which allowed exclusive and assignable control over athletes by the team that had originally signed them. Kuhn responded accordingly to Flood's letter: "Dear Curt: I certainly agree with you that you, as a human being, are not a piece of property to be bought and sold. That is fundamental in our society and I think obvious. However, I cannot see its application to the situation at hand."[7]

Syndicated columnist Jim Murray wrote, "The 'reserve clause,' to be sure, is just a fancy name for slavery. The only thing it doesn't let the owners do is flog the help. You can't flee over the ice, there's no underground railway. All you can do is pick up your glove and hum spirituals. You can wrap an old bandana around your head and call the boss 'Marse,' if you like. Lift the bat, chop that ball, git a little drunk and you land in sale." Murray then offered baseball some unsolicited advice: "I would try to keep that Flood right between its banks. Otherwise, when baseball sends those doves out, they may come back with salmon in their teeth. And every baseball park in America may have a sign 'No Game Tonight—On Account Of Flood.'"[8]

Red Smith reacted similarly, writing, "Thus the commissioner restates baseball's labor policy any time there is unrest in the slave cabins. 'Run along, sonny, you bother me.'" Undeterred by baseball's dismissiveness, Flood filed a federal lawsuit in New York against Kuhn and each of the major-league baseball clubs in January 1970. "I think the owners are underestimating me," he said. "They think I'm just trying to get more money for next season. They'll probably be taking it serious around March." Flood discussed the suit with Howard Cosell on *Wide World of Sports*.[9]

"It's been written, Curt, that you're a man who makes $90,000 a year," Cosell said, "which isn't exactly slave wages. What's your retort to that?"

"A well-paid slave is nonetheless a slave," Flood replied.[10]

In the *New York Amsterdam News*, the city's leading African American–owned paper, Dick Edwards wrote, "There are howls that baseball is dead if Flood wins his suit. That's tough, because if making the Lords obey one of the basic tenets upon which a democracy is built will kill baseball, it's time it was dead anyway."[11]

Flood sat out the 1970 season rather than play for the Phillies. He was eventually traded to the Washington Senators in time for the start of the 1971 season, but he had descended into full-blown alcoholism during his time away. Flood lasted only thirteen games with Washington before hopping a flight to Europe and abruptly retiring from baseball. His case eventually reached the US Supreme Court. In a 5-3 decision, the Court acknowledged that the antitrust exemption baseball enjoyed was an anomaly but declined to overturn its 1922 precedent.[12]

Flood lost his case, but he helped to expose the vast power imbalance between major-league teams and their players. Bolstered by the leverage that public awareness of the situation provided, Players Association executive director Marvin Miller orchestrated an arbitration victory three years later in which the arbitrator interpreted the reserve clause in major leaguers' contracts as enforceable only for one year. After Major League Baseball exhausted its appeals, owners and players compromised on a labor agreement that recognized free agency for players after six years with their original club. Over the following decade, average major-league salaries would jump more than eightfold. Today, eight-figure contracts for football, basketball, baseball, and hockey players in the United States are commonplace, as athletes continue to receive a more proportional piece of a steadily growing pie.

In the summer of 1970, after an exile from the sport of more than three years, Muhammad Ali won a federal court decision forcing the New York State Boxing Commission to reinstate his boxing license.[13] He returned to the ring that fall. After struggling to find a jurisdiction that would sanction him to fight, Ali finally received approval from Atlanta mayor Sam Massell—over the objection of Gov. Lester Maddox, who called for a boycott and declared an official day of mourning. Ali followed his third-round TKO of popular challenger Jerry Quarry with a December victory over Oscar "Ringo" Bonavena. Those wins paved the way for a championship bout at Madison Square Garden against undefeated Joe Frazier, who had captured the heavyweight championship in

Ali's absence. Though he would lose a unanimous decision to Frazier in the most highly anticipated fight of the era, Ali later recaptured the heavyweight title on two separate occasions, becoming the first three-time world heavyweight champion.

On June 28, 1971, the US Supreme Court overturned Ali's conviction for refusal to accept military induction. Justice John Marshall Harlan II had become convinced of the sincerity of Ali's conscientious objector claims, putting the eight justices in a 4–4 tie. (Thurgood Marshall recused himself because he had been solicitor general when the case began.) Justice Potter Stewart persuaded his judicial brethren to approve a compromise decision under which a unanimous court reversed Ali's conviction due to a legal error committed by the Justice Department in recommending to the Selective Service Appeal Board that Ali's conscientious objector claim should be denied.[14] Ali would go on to participate in some of the biggest sporting extravaganzas in history, expanding his global fame and notoriety to levels not previously imagined for an athlete.

Though he exhibited symptoms by the late 1970s, Ali would not be formally diagnosed with Parkinson's disease, presumably caused by injuries sustained in the ring, until 1984, three years after his retirement. As his tremors became more pronounced and speaking became more difficult, he limited his public appearances. But in 1996 Ali lit the Olympic torch with a quivering hand at the Games' opening ceremony in Atlanta. Nearly fifteen years after his last professional fight, Ali remained the most recognizable person in the world. A global television audience witnessed his last great public performance in one of the more indelible moments in Olympic history.

The public reaction to Ali's death in 2016 confirmed his status as a national hero, allaying any doubt that he had achieved a hallowed place in Americans' collective consciousness, or that the court of American public opinion had tacitly vindicated his once-controversial political positions. More than one hundred thousand people from across the country lined Louisville streets on a sunny June morning to witness the boxer's long funeral procession. Ali's casket traveled some twenty miles through the city, past his boyhood home, down Muhammad Ali Boulevard, and into Cave Hill Cemetery. After a private burial, foreign dignitaries, politicians including former president Bill Clinton, actors, musicians, religious leaders, athletes, and journalists from around the world were among the fifteen thousand filling Louisville's downtown sports arena for a public memorial service. The ceremony was broadcast on American television and streamed around the world. President Barack Obama expressed deep regret over his inability to attend due to his daughter's high school grad-

Muhammad Ali's funeral procession *passes in front of his boyhood home in Louisville, Ky., on June 10, 2016. Ali had been one of the most controversial public figures in the United States in the 1960s but was embraced as a national hero later in life. (AP Photo/Mark Humphrey, File)*

uation. Comedian Billy Crystal told the assemblage, "Ali forced us to take a look at ourselves. This brash young man thrilled us, angered us, confused us, challenged us, ultimately became a silent messenger of peace and taught us that life is best when you build bridges between people and not walls."[15]

Citing Ali as an inspiration, four of the NBA's biggest stars opened the ESPY sports awards telecast a month later with a call to action. Their remarks came in the wake of a pair of highly publicized fatal shootings of young black men by police officers and the subsequent killing of five police at a protest in Dallas. "We cannot ignore the reality of the current state of America," Carmelo Anthony of the New York Knicks said. "The system is broken. The problems are not new. The violence is not new. And the racial divide is not new. But the urgency to create change is at an all-time high."[16]

Los Angeles Clippers guard Chris Paul called on professional athletes to follow the example of a bygone generation of athletes, including Ali, Tommie Smith, John Carlos, and Arthur Ashe. Three-time NBA champion Dwayne Wade said of the violence and discord, "Enough. Enough is enough." Four-time league MVP LeBron James concluded, "I know tonight we're honoring Muhammad Ali, the GOAT [greatest of all time]. But to do his legacy any justice, let's use this moment as a call to action for all professional athletes to educate ourselves. Explore these issues. Speak up. Use our influence. And renounce all violence. And most importantly, go back to your communities, help rebuild them, help strengthen them, help change them. We all have to do better."[17]

Days later the Republican Party nominated Donald Trump for president. His acceptance speech echoed the dark themes and menacing messaging of Richard Nixon's address to the GOP convention in Miami Beach nearly fifty years earlier. Trump declared that the nation had reached "a moment of crisis" in which it was beset by "poverty and violence at home, war and destruction abroad." Then he promised to "restore law and order to our country."[18]

Notes

Introduction

1. Richard Rovere, "Freedom: Who Needs It," *Atlantic Monthly*, May 1968, 39; Associated Press, "Gallup Calls Public Disillusioned and Cynical," *New York Times*, February 10, 1968.

2. Scott Bixby, "Trump on Colin Kaepernick," *Guardian*, August 29, 2016.

3. Brian T. Smith, "49ers QB Colin Kaepernick Has Rights, But He's Not Correct," *Houston Chronicle*, August 27, 2016.

4. John Branch, "The Awakening of Colin Kaepernick," *New York Times*, September 7, 2017; Bryan Armen Graham, "Donald Trump Blasts NFL Anthem Protesters," *Guardian*, September 23, 2017; Mike Ayello, "VP Departs," *Indianapolis Star*, October 9, 2017. In February 2019, the NFL settled a grievance filed by Kaepernick under the league's collective bargaining agreement alleging that NFL owners had conspired to keep him out of the league. Though the terms were confidential, rumors that the settlement included a substantial payment to Kaepernick quickly surfaced.

5. Liam Stack, "The World Reacts on Social Media to Muhammad Ali's Death," *New York Times*, June 4, 2016.

Prologue

1. David Maraniss, *When Pride Still Mattered: A Life of Vince Lombardi* (New York: Simon and Schuster, 1999), 416; Edward Gruver, *Nitschke* (New York: Taylor, 2004), 173.

2. Bill Russell and Tyler Branch, *Second Wind: The Memoirs of an Opinionated Man* (New York: Random House, 1979), 111.

3. Jerry Kramer and Dick Schaap, *Instant Replay: The Green Bay Diary of Jerry Kramer* (New York: Doubleday, 1968), 266.

Chapter One

1. John W. Finney, "Dirksen Warns of 'Appeasement,'" *New York Times*, January 30, 1968; Kyle Longley, *LBJ's 1968: Power, Politics, and the Presidency in America's Year of Upheaval* (London: Cambridge University Press, 2018), 36. The *Pueblo* crisis would dog the Johnson administration for the rest of the year before the ship's crew was finally freed in late December. The ship itself remains in North Korean possession.

2. Rick Perlstein, *Nixonland: The Rise of a President and the Fracturing of America* (New York: Scribner, 2008), 227; Associated Press, "Major Describes Move," *New York Times*, February 8, 1968.

3. Jeff Shasol, *Mutual Contempt: Lyndon Johnson, Robert Kennedy, and the Feud that Defined a Decade* (New York: Norton, 1998), 414; UPI, "New Look Called For," *Minneapolis Star*, February 8, 1968; AP, "Vietnam Victory Not in Sight: RFK," *Nashville Tennessean*, February 9, 1968.

4. "Text of Nixon's Press Conference," *Los Angeles Times*, November 8, 1962.

5. Norman Mailer, *Miami and the Siege of Chicago: An Informal History of the Republican and Democratic Conventions of 1968* (New York: Random House, 2016), 36.

6. Joe McGinnis, *The Selling of the President* (New York: Penguin, 1988), 63.

7. Ben A. Franklin, "Wallace in Race; Will 'Run to Win,'" *New York Times*, February 9, 1968; Dan T. Carter, *The Politics of Rage: George Wallace, the Origins of New Conservatism, and the Transformation of American Politics* (Baton Rouge: LSU Press, 2000), 96.

8. Allen J. Matusow, *The Unraveling of America: A History of Liberalism in the 1960s* (Athens: University of Georgia Press, 2009), 425; Lewis L. Gould, *1968: The Election That Changed America* (Chicago: Ivan R. Dee, 2010), 61; David Farber, *Chicago '68* (Chicago: University of Chicago Press, 1988), 130; "Lecturing the Wrong Ones," *Alabama Journal*, September 23, 1968.

9. Mark Kerlansky, *1968: The Year that Rocked the World* (New York: Ballantine, 2004), 61.

10. Charles Kaiser, *1968 in America: Music, Politics, Chaos, Counterculture, and the Shaping of a Generation* (London: Weidenfield and Nicolson, 1988), 102; Don Oberdorfer, *Tet!: The Turning Point in the Vietnam War* (Baltimore: Johns Hopkins, 1971), 274–75.

11. Nick Thimmesch, "McCarthy Makes his Move," *Newsday*, December 2, 1967; Dominic Sandbrook, *Eugene McCarthy: The Rise and Fall of Postwar American Liberalism* (New York: Knopf, 2007), 117; "Dissenter on Vietnam: Eugene Joseph McCarthy," *New York Times*, October 17, 1967.

12. Doris Kearns Goodwin, *Lyndon Johnson and the American Dream* (New York: St. Martin's Griffin, 1991), 354; Myra MacPherson, "At Last a Party for McCarthy," *Boston Globe*, March 23, 1968; E. W. Kenworthy, "Senator Mixes Poetry with Politics," *Louisville Courier-Journal*, March 29, 1968. Not all McCarthy supporters favored peace. As many as 40 percent simply wanted a more effective American war effort rather than an end to hostilities.

13. Perlstein, *Nixonland*, 232.

14. Thurston Clarke, *The Last Campaign: Robert F. Kennedy and 82 Days That Inspired America* (New York: Henry Holt, 2008), 21; "Kennedy's Formal Text," *Nashville Tennessean*, March 17, 1968.

15. Tom Wicker, "Johnson Says He Won't Run," *New York Times*, April 1, 1968; Goodwin, *Lyndon Johnson and the American Dream*, 348; UPI, "RFK Doubts LBJ Victory," *Arizona Republic*, March 18, 1968.

16. Goodwin, *Lyndon Johnson and the American Dream*, 343.

17. Mike Wynn, "King's Visit to Augusta Brought Jubilation, Danger," *Augusta Chronicle*, March 23, 2008.

18. Nick Kotz, *Judgment Days: Lyndon Baines Johnson, Martin Luther King Jr., and the Laws That Changed America* (New York: Houghton Mifflin Harcourt, 2005), 409; Gould, *1968*, 34.

19. Jay Bowles, "Dr. King Indicated Premonition," *Louisville Courier-Journal*, April 5, 1968.

20. Kurlansky, *1968*, 117; Beate Kutschke and Barley Norton, eds., *Music and Protest in 1968* (New York: Cambridge University Press, 2013), 57; Kaiser, *1968 in America*, 148.

21. "Law and Order First," *Chicago Tribune*, April 7, 1968, quoted in Farber, *Chicago '68*, 143.

22. Ray E. Boomhower, *Robert F. Kennedy and the 1968 Primary Election* (Bloomington: Indiana University Press, 2008), 67–68.

23. Clarke, *Last Campaign*, 98.

24. Terence McArdle, "MLK Was Dead. Cities Were Burning. Could James Brown Keep Boston from Erupting, Too?" *Washington Post,* April 6, 2018; Curt Sampson, *The Lost Masters: Grace and Disgrace in '68* (New York: Atria, 2005), xvi.

25. Aram Goudsouzian, *King of the Court: Bill Russell and the Basketball Revolution* (Berkeley: University of California Press, 2010), 215.

26. Ibid., 151.

27. Richard Peterson, "The Baseball Season That Started Late," *Pittsburgh Post-Gazette*, January 21, 2013; Bob Gibson with Lonnie Wheeler, *Stranger to the Game: The Autobiography of Bob Gibson* (New York: Viking, 1994), 184.

28. Gibson with Wheeler, *Stranger to the Game*, 184–85.

29. Michael Gavin, *Sports in the Aftermath of Tragedy: From Kennedy to Katrina* (Lanham, MD: Scarecrow, 2012), 36; "Humphrey Sees Twins Win By 2–0," *New York Times*, April 11, 1968.

30. Jeremy D. Mayer, *Running on Race: Racial Politics in Presidential Campaigns, 1960–2000* (New York: Random House, 2002), 153; Anthony Lewis, "The Real Reagan," *New York Times*, October 24, 1983.

31. "Day of Mourning," *Chicago Tribune*, April 9, 1968.

32. Rebecca Burns, *Burial for a King: Martin Luther King Jr.'s Funeral and the Week That Transformed Atlanta and Rocked the Nation* (New York: Scribner, 2011), 158; Perlstein, *Nixonland*, 257.

33. Richard Severo, "Lester Maddox, Whites-Only Restaurateur and Georgia Governor, Dies at 87," *New York Times*, June 26, 2003; "Lester Maddox," *Guardian*, June 25, 2003; Burns, *Burial for a King*, 137.

34. Leigh Montville, *Sting Like a Bee: Muhammad Ali vs. The United States of America, 1966–1971* (New York: Doubleday, 2017), 196; William Drummond, "Open Housing Group Marches on Opponent," *Louisville Courier-Journal*, March 30, 1967.

35. Robert McG. Thomas Jr., "Howard Cosell, Outspoken Sportscaster on Television and Radio, Is Dead at 77," *New York Times*, April 24, 1995; Dave Kindred, *Sound and Fury: Two Powerful Lives, One Fateful Friendship* (New York: Free Press, 2006), 4, 180.

36. Jim Murray, "An Insult to the Game," *Los Angeles Times*, October 9, 1970;

Mark Ribowsky, *Howard Cosell: The Man, the Myth, and the Transformation of American Sports* (New York: Norton, 2012), 186.

37. Thomas Hauser, *Muhammad Ali: His Life and Times* (New York: Simon and Schuster, 1991), 143; Dave Kindred, *Sound and Fury*, 100.

38. "1-A Status Probably Won't Stop Title Bout," *Dayton Daily News*, February 18, 1966; "Title Fight Appears Certain," *Tampa Tribune*, February 19, 1966.

39. *New York Journal American*, February 22, 1966; Howard L. Bingham and Max Wallace, *Muhammad Ali's Greatest Fight: Cassius Clay vs the United States of America* (Lanham, MD: M. Evans, 2012), 114.

40. *Clay v. United States*, 397 F.22 901 (5th cir. 1968); Kindred, *Sound and Fury*, 103.

41. Hauser, *Muhammad Ali*, 167; Robert H. Boyle, "Champ in the Jug," *Sports Illustrated*, April 4, 1967.

42. Howard Cosell, "Ali Career Terminated by Non-Step," *Green Bay Press-Gazette*, October 25, 1973.

43. Bingham and Wallace, *Muhammad Ali's Greatest Fight*, 158.

44. "Boxing Bodies Go into Fast Ali Shuffle," *Chicago Tribune*, April 29, 1967.

45. Kindred, *Sound and Fury*, 122.

Chapter Two

1. Edwin O. Guthman and Jeffrey Shulman, eds., *RFK: Collected Speeches* (New York: Viking, 1993), 323–27.

2. Jack Newfield, *RFK: A Memoir* (New York: Nation Books, 2009), 233.

3. Guthman and Shulman, *RFK: Collected Speeches*, 327–30.

4. "The Brainwashed Candidate," *Time*, September 15, 1967; Andrew Johns, *Vietnam's Second Front: Domestic Politics, the Republican Party, and the War.* (Lexington: University Press of Kentucky, 2010), 166.

5. David Shaw, "Book Traces Actor's Career," *Long Beach Independent Press-Telegram*, May 25, 1968.

6. Linda Deutsch (Associated Press), "Reagans: Are They Like Couple Next Door?," *Appleton (WI) Post-Crescent*, July 13, 1980.

7. Ed Hayes, "Real Phonies Stand Up," *Orlando Evening Star*, April 10, 1968.

8. Curt Sampson, *The Masters: Golf, Money, and Power in Augusta, Georgia* (New York: Villard, 1999), 43–44.

9. Charles Fountain, *Sportswriter: The Life and Times of Grantland Rice* (New York: Oxford University Press, 2003), 6–7.

10. Herbert Warren Wind, "Rule 38, Paragraph 3," *New Yorker*, May 18, 1968, 125.

11. Jaime Diaz, "The Men the Masters Forgot," *Golf Digest*, April 1993; Sampson, *Masters*, 173–74. Under pressure from tour pros accustomed to their own caddies, Augusta National lifted the restriction in 1983. While the rule change reduced the contrast in complexions between the players and the men who toted their tools, it was not without its detractors. "In golf you don't see any more of this," Jariah "Bubba" Beard, who caddied for 1979 champion Fuzzy Zoeller, lamented as he pointed to his

dark skin. "The Monday of the Masters, I was somebody in this community," he said. Zoeller caused a stir in 1997 when he referred to that year's champion, Tiger Woods, as "little boy" and joked to reporters that Woods should not serve "fried chicken or collard greens or whatever the hell they serve" at the champion's dinner.

12. Frank Lett Sr., "Attention Golfers and All Good Sportsmen," *Michigan Chronicle*, February 24, 1968.

13. Jim Murray, "As White as the KKK," *Los Angeles Times*, April 6, 1969; Sampson, *Lost Masters*, 22. With a few exceptions, including the Masters, major professional sports were still a relative novelty in the Deep South. The Atlanta Falcons were entering their third season, as were the Atlanta Braves, having moved from Milwaukee in 1966.

14. "Jim Murray, Pulitzer-Winning Times Columnist Dies," *Los Angeles Times*, August 18, 1998.

15. Sampson, *Lost Masters*, 101.

16. Ron Firmite, "Nowhere to Hide," *Sports Illustrated*, October 14, 1990, says the debate was between a five or six iron.

17. Sampson, *Lost Masters,* 139.

18. Wind, "Rule 38, Paragraph 3"; "Isaac B. (Ike) Grainger, 104, An Expert on Golf's Rules," *New York Times*, October 14, 1999. According to a report in the *New Yorker* weeks later, Jones had wanted to find a precedent for leniency. Had he looked hard enough, or had enough time to do so, he would have had plenty from which to choose. Dow Finsterwald and Arnold Palmer had received lenient rulings at Augusta in the past decade, and British golf's ruling body had granted Bobby Locke clemency in a somewhat similar situation.

19. Sampson, *Lost Masters*, 156. There had been one foreign winner, in 1961, South African Gary Player.

20. Associated Press, "Goalby Has a Dream, Roberto a Nightmare," *Indianapolis Star*, April 15, 1968.

21. "So Much Pressure I Lose Brains," *Louisville Courier-Journal*, April 14, 1968; Alfred Wright, "Golf's Craziest Drama," *Sports Illustrated*, April 22, 1968.

22. Associated Press, "Own Stupidity Caused Error, De Vicenzo Says," *Philadelphia Enquirer,* April 15, 1968; David Moffit (UPI), "Goalby Is Regretful," *San Mateo (CA) Times*, April 15, 1968; "Loser 'Congratulations' Goalby and Remembers Brighter Side," *Louisville Courier-Journal*, April 14, 1968.

23. Sampson, *Lost Masters*, 175–77.

24. Associated Press, "Critics Call Masters Ruling 'Bum Deal,'" *Louisville Courier-Journal*, April 16, 1968.

25. Bill Beck, "Scorecard Rule Is Unfair, But Roberto Can Add, Too," *St. Louis Post-Dispatch*, April 16, 1968; Sampson, *Lost Masters,* 177–78.

26. Sampson, *Lost Masters*, 174; "The Friendly Game," *New York Times*, April 16, 1968.

27. Sampson, *Lost Masters*, xviii.

28. Richard Goldstein, "Roberto De Vicenzo, Victim of Golfing Gaffe, Dies at 94," *New York Times*, June 2, 2017.

29. Sampson, *Lost Masters*, 185–86.

30. Gould, *1968*, 66; "Humphrey Talks on Troop Policy," *York* (Pa.) *Gazette and Daily*, April 29, 1968.

31. Robert Stulberg, "Protesters Say They Will Not Negotiate Until CU Grants Disciplinary Amnesty," *Columbia Spectator*, April 24, 1968; Michael Stern, "Student Demonstrators Take Over Hamilton Hall," *Columbia Spectator*, April 24, 1968.

32. "Columbia Closes Campus After Disorders," *New York Times*, April 25, 1968; Douglas Martin, "Henry S. Coleman, 79, Dies," *New York Times*, February 4, 2008; "Protesters Crowd into Hamilton Hall for an All-Night Vigil," *Columbia Spectator*, April 24, 1968.

33. United Press International, "Strikers at Columbia Protest to Lindsay," *Indianapolis Star*, May 5, 1968.

34. Associated Press, "Procession for Derby Called Off," *Los Angeles Times*, May 2, 1967; Raymond Johnson, "Entry List for Derby Day Includes Big Police Force," *Nashville Tennessean*, May 3, 1967.

35. Douglas Robinson, "Protest at Derby Is Reported Off," *New York Times*, May 6, 1967; James E. "Ted" Bassett III and Bill Mooney, *Keeneland's Ted Bassett: My Life* (Lexington: University Press of Kentucky, 2009), 118.

36. "Jockey Won't Swerve to Miss Demonstrators," *Louisville Times*, May 3, 1967.

37. "Good Judgment," *Louisville Defender*, May 11, 1967; Gerald Henry, "The Infield Crowd Has Good Time Despite Drizzle," *Louisville Courier-Journal*, May 7, 1967.

38. "12th Pegasus Parade Witnessed by 200,000," *Louisville Courier-Journal*, May 3, 1968; "Heavyweight Champion Jimmy Ellis Named Marshal of Pegasus Parade," *Louisville Courier-Journal*, April 30, 1968.

39. Melvin Maddocks, "The Inner Life of a Wealthy Warrior," *Sports Illustrated*, May 23, 1977. Fuller's time as governor is perhaps most remembered for his controversial decision to deny clemency for Nicola Sacco and Bartolomeo Vanzetti, immigrant anarchists whose convictions for robbery and murder had garnered international attention.

40. Robert J. Clark, "Tiger Blood," *Thoroughbred Record*, April 27, 1968. Clark claimed that he conducted an informal survey at Bowie Racetrack in which he asked racegoers what Fuller should have done with the money that he gave to Mrs. King. The responses supposedly fell into three categories: "Why give it to Mrs. King?" 31 percent; "If Mr. Fuller wants to get rid of his money, he could have helped reimburse those who were deprived of property by rioters," 60 percent; "Mind your own business (or drop dead)," 9 percent.

41. Bob Hohler, "Thorns and Roses," *Boston Globe*, May 2, 2008; Douglas Martin, "Peter Fuller Dies at 89," *New York Times*, May 19, 2012; Dave Kindred, "From Soap Opera, A Derby Star!," *Louisville Courier-Journal*, May 2, 1968.

42. Jim Murray, "Derby Day at Churchill Downs Is Perfume and Mink," *Los Angeles Times*, May 5, 1968.

43. Marty McGee, "Alex Harthill Dead at 80," *Daily Racing Form*, July 15, 2005; Bill Christine, "The 1968 Kentucky Derby: The Victory That Wasn't, *Los Angeles Times*, May 1, 1988.

44. James Bolus, "The Alex Harthill Story," *Louisville Courier-Journal*, September 1, 1972; Jim Bolus, "Vet's Office Removed from Churchill Downs Barn," *Louisville Courier-Journal*, September 10, 1972.

45. Bill Christine, "Harthill Was Best Bet for Horses in Need," *Los Angeles Times*, July 24, 2005.

46. Kentucky lifted its ban in 1974.

47. Dave Kindred, "From Soap Opera, A Derby Star!," *Louisville Courier-Journal*, May 2, 1968.

48. Joe Hirsch, "Lavin's Imposts If Derby Were 'Cap,'" *Daily Racing Form*, May 4, 1968.

49. Molly McCormick, "The Julep Returns as Breakfast Fare," *Louisville Courier-Journal*, May 5, 1968; Associated Press, "'Another Kind of Race,' Nixon Remarks at Derby," *Cincinnati Enquirer*, May 5, 1968; Gould, *1968*, 63.

50. Jim Bolus, "Rider Asks 'Share' of Dancer's Image," *Louisville Courier-Journal*, May 5, 1968.

51. Herb Goldstein, "Bob Ussery 'Didn't Need Hunches' or Whip Either," *Daily Racing Form*, May 6, 1968; Jim Murray, "Derby Day at Churchill Downs Is Perfume and Mink," *Los Angeles Times*, May 5, 1968; Jobie Arnold, "Notes from Among the Roses," *Thoroughbred Record*, May 11, 1968.

52. Tom Easterling, "Great! Couldn't Dream It! Wonderful! Says Fuller," *Daily Racing Form*, May 6, 1968; Earl Ruby, "'Image' First to Go from Last to First Place Since Ponder," *Louisville Courier-Journal*, May 5, 1968; "Nixon Gets Into the Act," *St. Louis Post-Dispatch*, May 6, 1968.

53. Milton C. Toby, *Dancer's Image* (Charleston, SC: *History Press*, 2011), 63, 110; "Dancer's Derby Image Is Spoiled," *Cincinnati Enquirer*, May 8, 1968; Tom Easterling, "Pain-Killer Found in Urine Analysis," *Daily Racing Form*, May 8, 1968.

54. Whitney Tower, "A Bitter Pill," *Sports Illustrated*, May 20, 1968.

55. "Peter Fuller, owner of thoroughbred Dancer's Image, dies at 89," *Washington Post*, May 17, 2012; Tower, "Bitter Pill."

56. William Robertson, "Pick Up the Pieces, and Hold Up Your Head," *Thoroughbred Record*, May 18, 1968; Tower, "Bitter Pill."

57. Joe Hirsch, "Dancer's Image Case Remains Unresolved," *Daily Racing Form*, May 14, 1968. Without evidence of any specific wrongdoing, Cavalaris and Barnard were suspended for thirty days under the theory that trainers were strictly responsible for the condition of their animal.

58. "Kentucky Broadcasters Association Address, Lexington, May 21, 1968," in *The Public Papers of Louie B. Nunn, 1967–1971*, ed. Robert F. Sexton (Lexington: University Press of Kentucky, 1975), 137.

59. Associated Press, "Court Deprives Dancer's Image of '68 Derby Purse," *New York Times*, April 29, 1972; Hohler, "Thorns and Roses"; Christine, "The 1968 Kentucky Derby."

60. Jeff Frederick, *Stand Up for Alabama: Governor George Wallace* (Tuscaloosa: University of Alabama Press, 2007), x.

61. George Gallup, "Wallace Supporters Could Be a Threat," *Nashville Tennessean,* May 8, 1968.

Chapter Three

1. Clarke, *Last Campaign*, 50.

2. Associated Press, "Sen. Kennedy Expected Try on His Life," *Decatur (IL) Herald,* June 7, 1968.

3. Clarke, *Last Campaign*, 236–37.

4. Kaiser, *1968 in America*, 182.

5. Clarke, *Last Campaign*, 272; Evan Thomas, *Robert Kennedy: His Life* (New York: Simon and Schuster, 2002), 391.

6. United Press International, "A Newsman Gives Picture of Confusion," *Chicago Tribune,* June 6, 1968; Kyle Longley, *LBJ's 1968*, citing "FBI to Clark," The Personal Papers of Ramsey Clark, Box 123, LBJ Library.

7. Clarke, *Last Campaign*, 9; Joe McGinnis, "America the Ugly: Where Hate and Fear Create Vision of Hell," *Philadelphia Inquirer,* June 6, 1968.

8. Farber, *Chicago '68*, 99; Longley, *LBJ's 1968*, 143–44; Mike Royko, "The Untruth Hurts," *Boston Globe,* June 20, 1968.

9. Howard Cosell, *Cosell* (Chicago: Playboy Press, 1973), 360–61; John Florio and Ouisie Shapiro, *One Nation Under Baseball: How the 1960s Collided with the National Pastime* (Lincoln: University of Nebraska Press, 2017), 137.

10. Robert Lipsyte, "Teammates," *New York Times,* June 8, 1968.

11. Gibson with Wheeler, *Stranger to the Game*, 188.

12. Tim Wendel, *Summer of '68: The Season That Changed Baseball and America Forever* (New York: Da Capo, 2012), 47.

13. Milt Pappas with Wayne Mausser and Larry Names, *Out at Home: Triumph and Tragedy in the Life of a Major Leaguer* (Oshkosh, WI: Angel, 2000), 189–90.

14. Red Smith, "Baseball's Brass Further Tarnished," *Washington Post,* June 11, 1968; Associated Press, "Kennedy Aid Lauds Players," *St. Louis Post-Dispatch*, June 12, 1968.

15. Ron Briley, "Not So 'Young Ideas' on the Barricades in 1968," *Nine*, Vol.15, No.1 (Fall 2006): 52; Dick Young, "Soft Generals Never Last, Eckert Waned," *Chicago Tribune,* June 9, 1968; Sridhar Pappu, *The Year of the Pitcher: Bob Gibson, Denny McLain, and the End of Baseball's Golden Age.* (New York: Houghton Mifflin, 2017), 162; Red Smith, "Week-End of Shame," *Boston Globe,* June 10, 1968.

16. Mark Kriegel, "DiMaggio Was Perfect Fit for My Song, Simon Says," *New York Daily News,* November 27, 1998. The show aired April 8, 1970.

17. Jane Leavy, *The Last Boy: Mickey Mantle and the End of America's Childhood* (New York: Harper, 2010), 34; Ken Plutnicki, "Mantle's Knee Injury Was Just the Start," *New York Times,* May 4, 2012. In some retellings, Mantle stepped on an exposed drain cover. In others, it was a sprinkler head.

18. Arthur Daley, "Shotgun Overtones Disturbing," *Louisville Courier-Journal*, August 16, 1964.

19. Farber, *Chicago '68*, 17.

20. Jonah Raskin, *For the Hell of It: The Life and Times of Abbie Hoffman* (Berkley: University of California Press, 1997), 153.

21. Farber, *Chicago '68*, 188; Frank Kusch, *Battleground Chicago: The Police and the 1968 Democratic National Convention* (Chicago: University of Chicago Press, 2008), 107; "Police Repel Jeering Mob of Peaceniks," *Chicago Tribune*, August 26, 1968; "Bad Judgment by Police," *Waukesha* (Wis.) *Daily Freeman*, October 2, 1968.

22. Farber, *Chicago '68*, 314; Adam Cohen and Elizabeth Taylor, *American Pharaoh: Mayor Richard J. Daley—His Battle for Chicago and the Nation* (New York: Little, Brown, 2000), 474.

23. Lewis Chester, Godfrey Hodgson, and Bruce Page, *An American Melodrama* (New York: Viking, 1969), 583; Mailer, *Miami and the Siege of Chicago*, 177.

24. Kusch, *Battleground Chicago*, 102–3.

25. Jay Parini, *Empire of Self: A Life of Gore Vidal* (New York: Doubleday, 2015), 189; ibid.

26. Mike Royko, *Boss: Richard J. Daley of Chicago* (New York: Penguin, 1988), 189.

27. Chester, Hodgson and Page, *American Melodrama*, 592.

28. Arthur Miller, "The Battle of Chicago: From the Delegates' Side," *New York Times Magazine*, September 15, 1968; Austin Ranney, *Curing the Mischiefs of Faction: Party Reform in America* (Berkeley: University of California Press, 1976), 140.

29. "Arthur Ashe's Contribution," *New York Times*, September 15, 1968; "No Love Set," *New York Times*, August 29, 1968.

30. "Beauty Beholders Turn Critical Eye," *Minneapolis Star Tribune*, September 8, 1968; Megan Gibson, "The 'Bra Burning' Miss America Protest," *Time*, August 12, 2011.

31. Sidney Fine, *Violence in the Model City: The Cavanaugh Administration, Race Relations, and the Detroit Riot of 1967* (East Lansing: Michigan State University Press, 2007), 3.

32. "Decline in Detroit," *Time*, October 27, 1961; ibid., 41–46; Luke Bergmann, *Getting Ghost: Two Young Lives and the Struggle for the Soul of an American City* (Ann Arbor: University of Michigan Press, 2010), 54.

33. Fine, *Violence in the Model City*, 155–67.

34. Bill Dow, "Detroit '67: As Violence Unfolded, Tigers Played Two at Home vs. Yankees," *Detroit Free Press*, July 22, 2017.

35. Fine, *Violence in the Model City*, 177, 193.

36. Wendel, *Summer of '68*, 76.

37. Ibid., 87–88. A strike at Detroit's two major newspapers that lasted most of the season had the unlikely effect of further uniting the city around the Tigers. Fans who wanted news about their team had to tune into Ernie Harwell's radio broadcast.

38. Joe Falls, "Who'll Ever Forget the Mick's 535th?" *Detroit Free Press*, September 20, 1968; Leavy, *Last Boy*, 277–79; Florio and Shapiro, *One Nation Under*

Baseball, 148. According to other accounts, Mantle took two strikes before fouling off a third pitch. See Pappu, *Year of the Pitcher*, 237.

39. Leavy, *Last Boy*, 279.

40. Lou Smith, "Sound Off," *Cincinnati Enquirer*, January 15, 1969; Red Smith, "Mick Deserved McLain's Gift," *Boston Globe*, September 27, 1968.

41. Jack Berry, "Did Denny Give His Hero Parting Gift?," *Detroit Free Press*, September 20, 1968; Falls, "Who'll Ever Forget the Mick's 535th?"; *Minneapolis Star-Tribune*, September 20, 1968.

42. "Mantle Still Undecided," *Troy (NY) Record*, November 18, 1968.

43. Wendel, *Summer of '68*, 2; Gibson with Wheeler, *Stranger to the Game*, 165.

44. E. W. Kenworthy, "Nixon Campaigns in GOP Long Island," *Nashville Tennessean*, October 6, 1968. The Hall of Famers were Al Kaline, Eddie Mathews, Lou Brock, Steve Carlton, Orlando Cepeda, Bob Gibson, and St. Louis manager Red Schoendienst, who was inducted as a player.

45. "One Run Gives Red Sox First Game of Series," *New York Times*, September 6, 1918; Don Babwin, "1918 World Series Started U.S. Love Affair with National Anthem," *Chicago Tribune*, July 3, 2017.

46. David Zang, *Sports Wars: Athletes in the Age of Aquarius* (Fayetteville: University of Arkansas Press, 2001), 3–4.

47. Denny McLain, *I Told You I Wasn't Perfect* (Chicago: Triumph, 2007), 119.

48. Zang, *Sports Wars*, 5.

49. "Oh Say, Did You Hear?" *Detroit Free Press*, October 11, 1968; Barbara Stanton, "Storm Rages over Series Anthem," *Detroit Free Press,* October 8, 1968; Ernie Harwell, *Tuned to Baseball* (South Bend, Ind.: Diamond Communications, 1986), 125.

50. Pappu, *Year of the Pitcher*, 269.

51. Stanton, "Storm Rages over Series Anthem." The B side was an instrumental version of the Beatles' "And I Love Her" played by Feliciano on guitar.

52. Alex Belth, *Stepping Up: The Story of Curt Flood and His Fight for Baseball Players' Rights* (New York: Persea, 2006), 131.

53. Stuart L. Weiss, *The Curt Flood Story: The Man Behind the Myth* (Columbia: University of Missouri Press, 2007), 109.

54. Frank Lett Sr., "Hail the Champs," *Michigan Chronicle*, October 19, 1968.

55. Pappu, *Year of the Pitcher*, 287; Patrick Joseph Harrigan, *The Detroit Tigers: Club and Community, 1945–1995* (Toronto: University of Toronto Press, 1997), 123.

Chapter Four

1. Chester, Hodgson, and Page, *American Melodrama*, 432.

2. United Press International, "New Riot in Miami: Disturbances Spread, Three Negroes Killed," August 9, 1968. Nelson Rockefeller received 277 votes and Ronald Reagan 182, with various other candidates getting a smattering of support.

3. Chester, Hodgson, and Page, *American Melodrama*, 435; "Chamberlain Comes Out for Nixon," *Michigan Chronicle*, July 20, 1968.

4. "Let's Win This One for Ike," *Boston Globe*, August 9, 1968.

5. Michael A. Cohen, *American Maelstrom: The 1968 Election and the Politics of Division* (New York: Oxford University Press, 2016), 222.

6. John Underwood, "Games in Trouble," *Sports Illustrated*, September 30, 1968.

7. Richard Hoffer, *Something in the Air: American Passion and Defiance in the 1968 Mexico City Olympics* (New York: Simon and Schuster, 2009), 105, 109; "Tokyo Recessional," *Sports Illustrated,* November 4, 1964; Underwood, "Games in Trouble."

8. John Womack Jr., "Unfreedom in Mexico: Government Crackdown on the Universities," *New Republic*, October 12, 1968, 27; Hoffer, *Something in the Air*, 113.

9. Harry Giniger, "On an Embattled Campus, 8 Mexican Student Leaders Stress Moderate Aims," *New York Times*, September 23, 1968; Underwood, "Games in Trouble."

10. Kevin B. Witherspoon, "Protest at the Pyramid: The 1968 Mexico City Olympics and the Politicization of the Olympic Games" (PhD diss., Florida State University, 2003), 92; Carl J. Migdail, "An Olympic Eve—Biggest Flare-up Yet," *U.S. News and World Report*, October 14, 1968.

11. Amy Bass, *Not the Triumph but the Struggle: The 1968 Olympics and the Making of the Black Athlete* (Minneapolis: University of Minnesota Press, 2002), 32, quoting Harry Edwards, *The Revolt of the Black Athlete* (New York: Free Press, 1969), 101. San Jose State would become a university in 1972.

12. Douglas Hartmann, *Race, Culture, and the Revolt of the Black Athlete: The 1968 Olympic Protests and Their Aftermath*. (Chicago: University of Chicago Press, 2003), 49, citing *Nation*, November 6, 1967.

13. Hartmann, *Race, Culture, and the Revolt of the Black Athlete*, 54–55; Eric Kurhi, "Civil Rights Radical Harry Edwards Returns to San Jose State for Commencement," *Santa Cruz Sentinel*, May 28, 2016.

14. Hoffer, *Something in the Air*, 51.

15. Ibid., 56; Scott Moore, "Negroes to Boycott Olympics," *San Jose Mercury News*, November 24, 1967, 1. The workshop was part of the Black Youth Conference held at the Second Baptist Church.

16. "The Olympic Jolt: Hell No, Don't Go," *Life*, March 15, 1968, 22.

17. Ibid, 23.

18. John Underwood, "Triumph and Tragedy at Tahoe," *Sports Illustrated*, September 21, 1968; Hoffer, *Something in the Air*, 43; Kenny Moore, "A Courageous Stand," *Sports Illustrated*, August 5, 1991.

19. Moore, "Courageous Stand."

20. "Bad Mistake—Brundage," *San Jose Mercury News*, November 25, 1967; Bass, *Not the Triumph but the Struggle*, 92; Hartmann, *Race, Culture, and the Revolt of the Black Athlete*, 64; Robert Lipsyte, "Evidence Ties Olympic Taint to 1936 Games," *New York Times*, February 21, 1999.

21. Moore, "Negroes to Boycott Olympics."

22. Associated Press, "Owens Criticizes Negro Boycott," *Arizona Republic*, November 25, 1967; Associated Press, "Louis Frowns on Olympic Boycott," *New York Times*, April 3, 1968; Witherspoon, *Protest at the Pyramid*, 76–77.

23. Hartmann, *Race Culture, and the Revolt of the Black Athlete*, 65–66.

24. Harry Edwards, *The Revolt of the Black Athlete* (New York: Free Press, 1969), appendix E, 190–91.

25. "Should Negroes Boycott the Olympics?" *Ebony*, March 1968, 112; Bass, *Not the Triumph but the Struggle*, 136; Maynard Brichford, "Avery Brundage and Racism," *Global and Cultural Critique: Problematizing the Olympic Games*, Fourth International Symposium for Olympic Research 132 (1998); United Press International, "Boycott Hits Brundage," *Salem (OR) Journal,* December 15, 1967, 21.

26. Sam Goldaper, "Alcindor Clarifies TV Remark, Criticizes Racial Bias in U.S.," *New York Times*, July 23, 1968, 31.

27. Hoffer, *Something in the Air*, 66; Robert Lipsyte, "The Spirit of the Olympics," *New York Times*, August 1, 1968, 34; Witherspoon, *Protest at the Pyramid,* citing Arnold Hano, "The Black Rebel Who 'Whitelists' the Olympics," *New York Times Magazine*, May 12, 1968, 42–44.

28. Moore, "Courageous Stand"; Bob Ottum, "Dolls on the Move to Mexico," *Sports Illustrated*, September 2, 1968. The exclusion of women from the OPHR calls to mind the famous quote often attributed to Stokely Carmichael that the proper place for women in the Black Power movement was "prone."

29. Jonathan Rodgers, "A Step to an Olympic Boycott," *Sports Illustrated,* December 4, 1967; Witherspoon, *Protest at the Pyramid*, 78; "If They Run, They'll Win," *Ebony*, October 1968, 188; "Olympic Boycott?" *Newsweek*, December 4, 1967; "Negro Olympic Boycott is Off Target," *Life*, December 8, 1967, 4.

30. Moore, "Courageous Stand."

31. Hoffer, *Something in the Air*, 100; ibid.

32. Arthur Daley, "Amid Matchless Pageantry," *New York Times,* October 13, 1968.

33. Norman said that Smith and Carlos were receptive to his offer to support their cause. "They seemed delighted that I wanted one. Smith asked someone in the stands for his button. Carlos demanded it. He said. 'Hand that thing over,' and that's how I got my button." Over the years, stories revealed the button donor to be US rower Paul Hoffman. Bass, *Not the Triumph but the Struggle*, 245; "The Olympics' Extra Heat," *Newsweek*, October 28, 1968. Some published recollections, including John Carlos with Dave Zirin, *The John Carlos Story* (Chicago: Haymarket Books, 2011), 117–18, suggest that Norman acquired the button before the race.

34. Bass, *Not the Triumph but the Struggle*, 233; "U.S. Apologizes for Athletes, 'Discourtesy,'" *Los Angeles Times*, October 18, 1968; "The Eye of the Storm," *Sports Illustrated*, August 12, 1991.

35. Paul Zimmerman, "Blacks Take Their Stand," *New York Post*, October 17, 1968, quoted in Bass, *Not the Triumph but the Struggle*, 245.

36. "2 Accept Medals Wearing Black Gloves," *New York Times*, October 17, 1968; Carlos with Zirin, *John Carlos Story*, 117.

37. Cosell, *Cosell*, 58–59; Kindred, *Sound and Fury*, 145; *New York Times*, October 20, 1968.

38. Maureen Margaret Smith, "The 'Revolt of the Black Athlete:' Tommie Smith and John Carlos's 1968 Black Power Salute Reconsidered," in *Myths and Milestones in the History of Sport*, ed. Stephen Wagg (London: Palgrave Macmillan, 2011), 167.

39. Associated Press, "Action of Smith, Carlos Brings Apology, Threat From USOC," *Albuquerque Journal*, October 18, 1968; Red Smith, "Black Beret, Clenched Fist," *Rochester (NY) Democrat and Chronicle*, October 20, 1968.

40. "The Olympics' Extra Heat," *Newsweek*, October 28, 1968, 79; Paul Zimmerman, "The Protest," *New York Post*, October 19, 1968; "Some Negro Athletes Threaten to 'Go Home' Along With Smith and Carlos," *New York Times*, October 19, 1968.

41. John Bloom, *There You Have It: The Life, Legacy, and Legend of Howard Cosell* (Amherst: University of Massachusetts Press, 2010), 81; *ABC Evening News*, October 18, 1968.

42. "U.S. Suspends Pair," *New York Post*, October 18, 1968; Bass, *Not the Triumph but the Struggle*, 269.

43. "Black Olympians Given No Hearing, Muskie Declares," *Chicago Daily Defender*, October 22, 1968; "National Anthem Only for Whites Says Carlos," *St. Louis Post-Dispatch*, October 27, 1968; "Jesse Owens Maintains Smith and Carlos Were Not Treated Unfairly," *Michigan Chronicle*, November 23, 1968.

44. "Letters: Black Power and the Olympic Games," *New York Times*, October 23, 1968; "Olympic Committee Quits 'Making Ado' about Balled Fists," *Pittsburgh Courier*, November 2, 1968.

45. Frank R. Saunders, "The Memory Lingers On," *Michigan Chronicle*, November 2, 1968.

46. Brad Pye Jr., "Olympics Not Platform for Problems," *Los Angeles Sentinel*, October 24, 1968.

47. Brent Musburger, "Bizarre Protest by Smith, Carlos Tarnish Medals," *Chicago American*, quoted in Dave Zirin, "After Forty-Four Years, It's Time Brent Musburger Apologized to John Carlos and Tommie Smith," *Nation*, June 4, 2012. Musburger would move from the *Chicago American* on to bigger stages, becoming a leading sports broadcaster for CBS and ABC.

48. Bloom, *There You Have It*, 81–82; *ABC Evening News*, October 25, 1968.

49. Hartmann, *Race, Culture and the Revolt of the Black Athlete*, 171.

Chapter Five

1. James Charles Cobb, *Redefining Southern Culture: Mind and Identity in the Modern South* (Athens: University of Georgia Press, 1999), 70.

2. Chester, Hodgson, and Page, *American Melodrama*, 661.

3. Ibid., 699.

4. See Peter Baker, "Nixon Tried to Spoil Johnson's Vietnam Peace Talks in '68, Notes Show," *New York Times*, January 3, 2017.

5. Lawrence Linderman, "*Playboy's* Candid Conversation with the Super Swinger QB, Joe Namath," *Playboy*, December 1969; James Reston, "Joe Namath, the New Anti-Hero," *New York Times*, August 21, 1971.

6. Mark Kriegel, *Namath: A Biography* (New York: Penguin, 2004), 59.

7. Ibid., 71.

8. Jim Murray, "'Bama in the Balkans," *Los Angeles Times*, December 4, 1964.

At that time, an Associated Press poll conducted at the end of the regular season determined the national championship.

9. Joe Willie Namath and Dick Schapp, *I Can't Wait Until Tomorrow 'Cause I Get Better Looking Every Day* (New York: Random House, 1969), 202.

10. Arthur Daley, "Philosophy of a Spender," *New York Times*, January 10, 1965.

11. Namath and Schapp, *I Can't Wait Until Tomorrow 'Cause I Get Better Looking Every Day*, 204; Daley, "Philosophy of a Spender."

12. Randy Roberts and Ed Krzemienski, *Rising Tide: Bear Bryant, Joe Namath and Dixie's Last Quarter* (New York: Hachette, 2013), 344.

13. Ibid., 395.

14. Robert Markus, "The Other Side of Sweet Joe Namath," *Chicago Tribune*, September 7, 1967; Allison Danzig, "No. 1 Team Is Stopped on One-Foot Line," *New York Times*, January 2, 1965; Bobby Hawthorn, *Longhorn Football: An Illustrated History.* (Austin: University of Texas Press, 2007), 122.

15. Morris McLemore, "Joe Namath Strikes It Rich," *Miami News*, January 3, 1965; Dave Anderson, "Making It," *New York Times*, February 1, 1969.

16. Arthur Daley, "It's Only Money," *New York Times*, January 4, 1965; Dick Young, "Young Ideas," *New York Daily News*, January 3, 1965.

17. Robert H. Boyle, "Showbiz Sonny and His Quest for Stars," *Sports Illustrated*, July 19, 1965.

18. Kriegel, *Namath*, 164.

19. Dan Jenkins, "The Sweet Life of Swingin' Joe," *Sports Illustrated*, October 17, 1966.

20. Dave Anderson, "Jets' 'Golden Arm' Joe Namath May Be Playing for Uncle Sam," *New York Journal-American*, August 11, 1965.

21. United Press International, "Army Gives Full Facts on Namath," *St. Louis Times-Dispatch*, December 8, 1965.

22. "Namath's 4-F Knee: The Army Punts," *New York Herald-Tribune,* December 9, 1965.

23. Jenkins, "Sweet Life of Swingin' Joe"; Associated Press, "Mantle Rejected for Draft Again," *New York Times*, November 4, 1952.

24. Dave Anderson, "Could Swinging Joe Namath Make It in the Tough NFL?," *True Magazine,* September 1968; Kriegel, *Namath*, 170.

25. Ed Gruver, *The American Football League: A Year by Year History* (Jefferson, NC: MacFarland, 1997), 199; Harrigan, *Detroit Tigers*, 160; Arthur Daley, "$onny, Money, and Merger," *New York Times*, January 6, 1967.

26. Jimmy Breslin, "Namath All Night Long," *New York Magazine*, April 7, 1969; Kriegel, *Namath,* 335; Associated Press, "Half of FBI Recruits are Vietnam War Vets," *Arizona Republic*, December 9, 1970.

27. William Wallace, "Trading of Namath is Suggested to Solve Friction with Jets," *New York Times*, August 15, 1968.

28. Kriegel, *Namath*, 237–38.

29. Ibid., 242.

30. Stephen Hanks, *The Game That Changed Pro Football* (New York: Birch Lane, 1989), 68; Kriegel, *Namath*, 245.

31. "Namath Takes It off—At $10 a Clip," *New York Times*, December 12, 1968.

32. Dave Anderson, "Jets Find Role of 17-Point Underdogs Unfitting," *New York Times*, January 3, 1969.

33. Michael Oriard, *Brand NFL: Making and Selling America's Favorite Sport* (Chapel Hill: University of North Carolina Press, 2010), 39.

34. Kriegel, *Namath*, 260–61; Jack Hand (Associated Press), "Namath Is His Own Man," *Louisville Courier-Journal*, June 7, 1969; "Report of Fight Denied by Namath," *New York Times*, January 8, 1969.

35. United Press International, "Joe's Moment of Truth Is Here," *Indianapolis Star*, January 12, 1969.

36. Luther Evans, "'I Guarantee We'll Win'—Namath," *Miami Herald*, January 10, 1969. Sportswriter Dave Anderson was in attendance for the guarantee and recalled Namath's statement as follows: "You can be the greatest athlete in the world, but if you don't win those football games, it doesn't mean anything. And we're going to win Sunday, I'll guarantee you." Dave Anderson, *Countdown to Super Bowl* (New York: Random House, 1969), 163.

37. Larry Merchant, *And Every Day You Take Another Bite* (Garden City, NY: Doubleday, 1971), excerpted in *Philadelphia Daily News*, November 4, 1971. His estimates of the size of the television audience were exaggerated.

38. Bloom, *There You Have It*, 80.

Epilogue

1. White House Special Files, Staff Member and Office Files, President's Office Files, Annotated News Summaries, June 1969, Nixon Presidential Materials, National Archive at College Park, Maryland, cited in Kriegel, *Namath*, 297.

2. Maraniss, *When Pride Still Mattered*, 496.

3. Pete Axthelm, "The Great National Bore," *Newsweek*, October 14, 1968, quoted in Hiley Ward, "Wild Rejoicing But a Dull Sport," *Detroit Free Press*, October 12, 1968.

4. Weiss, *Curt Flood Story*, 157.

5. Brad Snyder, *A Well Paid Slave: Curt Flood's Fight for Free Agency in Professional Sports* (New York: Penguin, 2007), 68.

6. Ed Edmonds and Frank G. Houdek, *Baseball Meets the Law: A Chronology of Decisions, Statutes and Other Legal Events* (Jefferson, NC: McFarland, 2017), 118.

7. *Federal Baseball Club v. National League*, 259 U.S. 200 (1922); *Flood v. Kuhn*, 407 U.S. 258 (1972); Martin Appel, *Hardball: The Education of a Baseball Commissioner* (Lincoln: University of Nebraska Press, 1997), 83.

8. Jim Murray, "The Curt Flood Case: Lift That Bat, Chop That Ball," *Los Angeles Times*, January 21, 1970.

9. Ira Berkow, *Red: A Biography of Red Smith* (Lincoln: University of Nebraska

Press, 2007), 204; Associated Press, "Flood Planning Strategy," *Cincinnati Enquirer*, January 3, 1970.

10. Snyder, *Well-Paid Slave*, 104.

11. Abraham Iqbal Khan, *Curt Flood in the Media: Baseball, Race, and the Demise of the Activist Athlete* (Oxford: University Press of Mississippi, 2012), 146.

12. *Flood v. Kuhn*, 407 U.S. 258 (1972).

13. *Ali v. Athletic Com'n*, 316 F. Supp. 1246 (S.D.N.Y. 1970).

14. *Clay v. United States*, 430 U.S. 698 (1971). The Justice Department had provided three reasons for its recommendation, including its determination that Ali's pacifist beliefs were not religiously based and were not sincerely held. The DOJ later conceded that Ali's beliefs were, in fact, religiously based and sincerely held. The Appeals Board still could have denied Ali's appeal based on a determination that he was not actually opposed to war in *any* form, but the Board did not specify upon which grounds it based its denial. Therefore, the Supreme Court held, "there [was] absolutely no way of knowing upon which of the three grounds offered in the Department letter it relied."

15. Associated Press, "World Bids Farewell to Boxing Great," *Chicago Tribune*, June 12, 2016.

16. Scott Cacciola, "Carmelo Anthony Is Using His Voice," *New York Times*, July 19, 2016.

17. Shannon Ryan, "Athletes' Voices Coming Through," *Chicago Tribune*, July 19, 2016.

18. David Smith, "Trump's Republican Convention Speech," *Guardian*, July 22, 2016.

Index

Page numbers in **boldface** refer to illustrations.

Aaron, Tommy, 38–40
Adams, Eddie, 8–9
Ailes, Roger, 10–11
Alcindor, Lew, 90
Ali, Muhammad: childhood, 24–25; college speaking tour, 29–30; and Cosell, 25–26, 28–**29**; and Department of Justice, 27–28; and the draft, 24, 26–27; Edwards demands titles returned, 89; funeral, 126–**27**; and King, 24; Liston fight, **25**; Olympic torch ceremony, 126; opposition to Vietnam War, 27–28, 30; Parkinson's disease, 126; referenced by Trump, 4; refuses military induction, 28; reinstatement and return to the ring, 125–26; sentenced to prison, 24; stripped by NYSAC, 29; support for George Wallace, 24; WBA championship, 45
American Broadcasting Company (ABC): and Cosell, 25, 99, 120; Democratic convention coverage, 64; and Olympics, 95–96, 99; Vidal-Buckley conflict, 66
American Football League (AFL), 108–9, 114, 117
Anthony, Carmelo, 127
Ashe, Arthur, 69–70, 128
Auerbach, Red, 20
Augusta National Golf Club, 34–37, 40–42

Baltimore Colts, 110, 117–20
Boston, Ralph, 91
Boston Celtics, 19–20
Boston Red Sox, 74, 78
Breathitt, Edward T., 45
Breslin, Jimmy, 56

Brock, Lou, 76, 137n44
Brown, "Crosshanded" Henry, 38
Brown, James, 19, 34
Brundage, Avery, 83, **87**, 88–89, 96, 98–99
Buchanan, Patrick, 10
Buckley, William F., 66
Butazolidin ("Bute"), 49, 51–52, 74, 115

caddies, 34, 36, 38–40, 132n11
Calumet Farm, 46–48, 50
Carlos, John, 86–87, 92–**93**, 94–98
Carmichael, Stokely, 16, 52, 139n28
Caummisar, Basil, 45
Cavalaris, Lou, 46, 49, **51**, 135n57
Cavanagh, Jerome, 71
Chamberlain, Wilt, 20, 23, 82
Chennault, Anna, 104
Chicago Cubs, 78
Chicago Defender, 88
Chicago Tribune, 18, 22, 64, 98
Churchill Downs, 44–45, 48, 50–52
Cincinnati Reds, 60
Clay, Cassius. *See* Muhammad Ali
Clemente, Roberto, 21
Columbia Broadcast Systems (CBS), 11, 47, 64, 68, 96, 141n47
Columbia University, 43–44
Conrad Hilton Hotel, 64–67
Cosell, Howard: and Ali, 25–26, 28–**29**; and coverage of Olympics, 95–97, 99; interview of Curt Flood, 124; speaks of Robert Kennedy's death, 59; Super Bowl III prediction, 118, 120
Cronkite, Walter, 11–12, 25, 52, 66

Daley, Arthur, 62, 92, 110, 114
Daley, Richard J., 16, 18–19, 62–64, 67–68
Dallas Cowboys, 5–6
Dancer's Image (horse), 45–**51**, 52–53

De Vicenzo, Roberto, 37–39, **40**–43
Democratic National Convention, 63–68
demonstrations. *See* protests
Detroit riots, 71–**72**
Detroit Tigers, 70–80
Dick Cavett Show, 61
DiMaggio, Joe, 61, 109
Drysdale, Don, 57

Eckert, William "Spike," 21, 60, 73, 75, 124
Edwards, Harry, 84–87, 89–92
Eisenhower, Dwight, 9
Ellis, Jimmy, 45
Eubank, Weeb, 116
Evans, Lee, 86, 88, 92

Feliciano, Jose, **77**, 78–79
Flood, Curt, 79–80, 121–22, **123**, 124–25
Forward Pass (horse), 46–47, 50
Freehan, Bill, 79
Fuller, Alvan Tufts, 46–48, 134n39
Fuller, Peter, 46–49, **51**–53, 134n40

Gallup, George, 1, 53, 129n1, 135n61
Gibson, Bob, 21, 59, 74–**76**, 79
Goalby, Bob, 38–**40**, 41–43
Goldwater, Barry, 49
Gowdy, Curt, 119–20
Grainger, Ike, 39
Grant Park, 64–66
Green Bay Packers, 5–6
Greene, Charlie, 91
Greenspan, Alan, 10

Harthill, Alex, 48–50, 52
Harvard crew, 90, 94
Harwell, Ernie, 71, 77–80, 137n37
Hoffman, Abbie, 63
Horton, Willie, 71, 79
Houk, Ralph, 74
Houston Astros, 21, 60
Howell, Bailey, 20
Humphrey, Hubert H.: announces candidacy for presidential election, 43;
attends King funeral, 23; and Chicago
convention, 63, 66–68; congratulates
Bob Gibson, 75–**76**; criticizes student
demonstrations, 44; presidential campaign, 82, 101–4; throws first pitch, 22
Huntley, Chet, 65

Ice Bowl, 5–6
Ingraham, Judge Joe, 29
Institute for Defense Analyses, 43–44
International Olympic Committee
   (IOC), 87, 89, 96, 98–99

Jackson, Carl, 40
James, Larry, 92
James, LeBron, 128
Johnson, Jack, 3
Johnson, Lyndon: decision not to seek
   reelection, 14–15; responds to Bobby
   Kennedy's death, 58–59; signing Civil
   Rights Act of 1968, **14**; and State of
   the Union address, 7
Jones, Robert Tyre "Bobby" Jr., 34–37,
   39, 42, 133n18
Jones, Warner L. Jr., 48

Kaepernick, Colin, 3–4
Kennedy, Jackie, 6, 55, 57, 97
Kennedy, John F., 6, 9, 107
Kennedy, Joseph P., 119
Kennedy, Robert: announces presidential candidacy, 13–15; assassination,
   57–59; Democratic primary campaigns, 31–32, 55–56, **58**; funeral and
   public reaction to his death, 58–61;
   GNP speech, 32; Indianapolis speech
   following King's death, 19; at King's
   funeral, 23; opposes Johnson's war
   policy, 8
Kennedy, Ted, 67, 119
Kentucky Derby, 44–52
Kentucky State Racing Commission, 53
Kerner Commission, 15
King, A.D. Williams, 45

King, Coretta Scott, 46–48, 51–52, 57
King, Martin Luther Jr.: address at
    National Cathedral, 15; assassination,
    16; Beulah Baptist Church speech,
    15; final public speech, 16; funeral,
    23; and Harry Edwards, 89; public
    reaction to death, 16–23
Kramer, Jerry, 6
Ku Klux Klan, 10, 45
Kuhn, Bowie, 124

Lambeau Field, 5, **6**
LeMay, Gen. Curtis E., 103
Lewis, John, 57
Lindsay, John, 56
Liston, Sonny, **26**
Lolich, Mickey, 72–73, 75, 78–79
Lombardi, Vince, 5–6, 114–15, 118, 121–22
Los Angeles Times, 25, 37, 47, 80, 94
Louis, Joe, 3, 88
Louisville Courier-Journal, 45, 49
Louisville Defender, 45

Maddox, Lester, 23, 125
Madison Square Garden, 89, 125
Mantle, Mickey, 61–**62**, 63, 73–74, 114,
    118, 121
Maris, Roger, 79–80
Masters golf tournament, 34–43
Mays, Willie, 61
McCarthy, Eugene, 12–13, 56, 64–68
McCarver, Tim, 21
McLain, Denny, 73–76, 78, 80
Memphis sanitation workers' strike, 16
Mercein, Chuck, 6
Merchant, Larry, 120
Mexico City Olympics: concerns
    regarding infrastructure, 82–83;
    men's 200 meter finals and medal
    ceremony, 92–**93**, 94–95; opening
    ceremony, 92; protests before the
    start of the games, 83–84; reaction to
    Smith and Carlos, 96–99; television
    coverage, 96

Michaels, Lou, 118–19
Michigan Chronicle, 37, 70–71, 80, 98
Mike Douglas Show, 10
Miller, Arthur, 68
Minnesota Twins, 22
Miss America Pageant, 70
Morgan, Robin, 70
Muhammad, Elijah, 28
Mundt, Karl E., 8
Murphy, Isaac, 50
Murray, Jim, 25, 37, 47, 108, 124
Musburger, Brent, 98–99
Muskie, Edmund, 97
"My Old Kentucky Home" (song), 47, 50

Namath, Joe: business ventures, 115,
    121; childhood, 106; collegiate career,
    107–8; contract negotiations, 108–9;
    Heidi game, 116; impact on AFL,
    114–15; knee troubles, 110, 113, 115,
    118, 121; military draft status, 113–14;
    non-partisanship, 106; off-field life-
    style, 111–13, 115; Orange Bowl, 109–10;
    recruitment to Alabama, 106–7;
    Super Bowl, **111**, 117–20
Nation of Islam, 26, 28
national anthem. *See* "Star Spangled
    Banner"
National Association for the Advance-
    ment of Colored People (NAACP),
    10, 70
National Broadcasting Company
    (NBC): AFL broadcast deal, 108, 114;
    coverage of Democratic National
    Convention in Chicago, 65; coverage
    of George Wallace, 101; coverage of
    Humphrey foreign policy speech; Fe-
    liciano national anthem performance
    and public reaction, 78; *Heidi* game,
    117; interview with Lew Alcindor, 90;
    Joe Namath's significance to AFL
    broadcasts; Super Bowl III coverage,
    119–20; Vietnam War editorial, 12;
    World Series coverage, 78

National Football League (NFL), 3–6, 108–9, 114, 121

New York Daily News, 41, 61, 74, 110, 133n22

New York Jets, 108–11, 118–22

New York Mets, 60–61, 108

New York State Athletic Commission (NYSAC), 28–29

New York Times, 12, 42, 59, 69, 92, 110, 115

New York Yankees, 61–62, 71, 73–74, 118

Nguyen Ngoc Loan, **9**

Nicklaus, Jack, 37, 41, 133n22

Nitschke, Ray, 5

Nixon, Richard Milhous: announces presidential candidacy, 9–10; attends King's funeral, 23; campaign for Republican nomination, 32–33; criticizes student protests, 44; inaugurated, 120; Joe Namath on enemies list, 115, 121; at Kentucky Derby, 49–51; at Orange Bowl, 109; at Republican convention, 81–82, 128; throwing first pitch, 105; wins presidential election, 104; and World Series, 75

Norman, Peter, **93**–95

North Korea, 7, 129n1

Nunn, Louie B., 49–51, 53

Oakland Raiders, 5–6, 114, 116–17

Ohlmeyer, Don, 25

Olympic Games. *See* Mexico City Olympics

Olympic Project on Human Rights (OPHR), 89–91, 94–95, 139n28

Ordaz, Gustavo Diaz, 82, 92

Owens, Jesse, 3, 88, 91, 97–98, 140n43

Palmer, Arnold, 37, 41, 133n18

Pappas, Milt, 60

Paul, Chris, 128

Pegasus Parade, 44–45

Pence, Mike, 4

Pepitone, Joe, 73

phenylbutazone. *See* Butazolidin

Philadelphia 76ers, 19–20

Pittsburgh Courier, 98

Pittsburgh Pirates, 21

Player, Gary, 37

Price, Jim, 73

protests: Columbia University, 43–44; at Democratic National Convention, 63–**65**, 66–68; at Kentucky Derby, 44–45; in Mexico City, 83–84; Smith and Carlos at Olympics, 92–**93**, 94–97

Rather, Dan, 66

Ray, James Earl, 16

Reagan, Ronald, 22, 33, 58, 82, 85

Republican National Convention, 81–82

reserve clause, 124–25

Ribicoff, Abraham, **67**

Rice, Grantland, 34–35

riots: in Detroit, 70–72; following King's assassination, 16, **17**–**18**, 19, 22; in Mexico City, 82–83; in Miami, 81

Roberts, Charles de Clifford "Cliff" Jr., 34–**36**, 37, 41–42

Robinson, Jackie, 3, 23, 75, 97

Rockefeller, Nelson, 33, 138n2

Romary, Janice-Lee, 92

Romney, George, 32, 71, 79

Rozelle, Pete, 121

Rubin, Jerry, 63

Russell, Bill, 5, 20, 23, 59

Ruth, Babe, 35, 73, 78, 109

San Francisco Giants, 60

San Jose State University track team, 84–85, 87–88

Schmeling, Max, 3

Screen Actors Guild, 33

Scully, Vin, 59

Seagren, Bob, 97

Shula, Don, 118–19

Sifford, Charlie, 36–37

Simon, Paul, 61

Simpson, O.J., 90, 121
Sirhan, Sirhan Bishara, 57
Smith, Red, 60–61, 73, 96, 124
Smith, Tommie, 85–86, 88, 92–**93**, 94–98
Southern Christian Leadership Conference (SCLC), 18, 24, 45
Spindletop Hall, 49–50
Sports Illustrated: Kentucky Derby coverage, 52; Olympic coverage, 82–83, 86, 91; reports on Namath, 110, 112, 114; Sportsman of the Year award to Russell, 20
St. Louis Cardinals, 21, 59, 74–76, 78–79, 122
Starr, Bart, 5–6, 82, 120
"Star-Spangled Banner, The," 77–79, 94
Summerall, Pat, 39

Tet Offensive, 8
Thoroughbred Record, 47, 52
Tokyo Olympics, 83
Trump, Donald, 3–4, 128
Tyus, Wyomia, 91, 95

Unitas, Johnny, 110, 119–20
United States Olympic Committee (USOC), 96–97
United States Supreme Court, 29, 124–26, 143n14
University of Alabama, 10–**11**, 106–8, 110
U.S. Open (tennis), 69–70
USS *Pueblo*, 7–8, 128n1
Ussery, Bobby, 46, 50–**51**

Valenzuela, Milo, 50–51
Vidal, Gore, 66
Viet Cong, 8, **9**, 11, 30

Wade, Dwayne, 128
Wagner, Dick, 60
Wallace, George: announces presidential candidacy, 10; appeal to northern whites, **102–3**; endorsed by police, 11; late surge in polls, 82, 101; and obstruction of integration of University of Alabama, **11**, 107; at Orange Bowl, 109; responds to hecklers, **102**; supported by Muhammad Ali, 24;
Wallace, Lurleen, 53
Wallace, Mike, 66
Washington D.C. riots, 16–**18**
Washington Post, 22, 42
Werblin, Sonny, 108–10, 114–15
Westmoreland, Gen. William, 8, 12
Winkfield, Jimmy, 50
Winter, Lloyd "Bud," 84, 87–88
World Series, 74–80

Youth International Party ("Yippies"), 63–64